June 12, 2022

Rabbi Potash.

Thank you for attending the J Reuben Clark law Society session honoring Robert Abrams. I was blessed to be assigned to sit next to you — very glad that we met.

Thanks for accepting my invitation to read this book. "Behold how good and how pleasant it is for brethren to dwell together in unity!"

Psalms 133

I look forward to receiving your comments —

With love & respect

Joseph Jarvis MS MSPH
1373 Perrys Hollow Drive, SLC UT 84103
801 633 0613
joseph.jarvis@msn.com

THE
HOPE OF THE
PROMISE

ISRAEL IN ANCIENT AND LATTER DAYS

DR. JOSEPH Q. JARVIS

Photographs by Elizabeth Q. Stewart
& Dr. Joseph Q. Jarvis

Editorial work by Eschler Editing
Cover design by Brian Halley
Interior print design and layout by Kristy S. Gilbert
Ebook design and layout by Kristy S. Gilbert
Production services facilitated by E&E Books

Published by Scrivener Books
978-1-949165-28-9 (paperback)
978-1-949165-29-6 (hardcover)

*Dedicated to Gordon and Carol Madsen, who first
brought me to the Holy Land, and to Nir
and Hanna Ganon Nitzan, my Israeli friends
and trip organizers*

TABLE OF CONTENTS

INTRODUCTION

The Bible is a startling book. Its assertions about the human condition are revolutionary. In the Bible we read of men and women like you and me—mortal and sometimes good but often doubting, envious, argumentative, or otherwise fraught with human failings—who come to know God and rejoice in His mercy.

In the opening book of the Bible, we meet Jacob, who has cunningly stolen the birthright from his brother Esau. Years later, he fears Esau will make it impossible for him to peacefully settle in their home territory. He brings that fear to God: "O God of my father Abraham, and God of my father Isaac. . . . I am not worthy of the least of all thy mercies. . . . Deliver me, I pray thee, from the hand of my brother . . . for I fear him" (Genesis 32:9–11). Overnight, in apparent answer to that prayer, Jacob meets God, wrestles with Him, and presumes to claim a blessing. He is renamed Israel, which means "one who prevails with God." The next day, Jacob (or Israel) meets Esau, who "[runs] to meet him, and [embraces] him, and [falls] on his neck, and [kisses] him: and they [weep]" (Genesis 33:4).

That's the surprise message in the Bible. Unworthy men and women, like

Jacob, can bring their fears to God and prevail upon Him to help them. If we incline ourselves to God, if we wrestle with our relationship with the Almighty, we too can be included in the house of Israel, the family of God's children who prevail with God.

The Bible is an account of God's dealings with mankind as seen through His covenants and promises to the house of Israel. He is Jehovah in the Old Testament and Jesus in the New Testament, and His promises to Israel are extended to all who in any manner lean into a relationship with Him, take Him at His word, and try to follow Him no matter their color, culture, gender, age, socioeconomic status, or when in the course of human history they lived upon the earth.

As He did as Jehovah during Old Testament times, Jesus invites all His brothers and sisters to come unto Him and prevail with God; in other words, to join the house of Israel. He promises peace and joy in this life no matter the suffering, dilemmas, or hardships we must endure. These promises are extended from the first page of Genesis to the last page of Revelations. It is up to us to read about them, understand them, and embrace them by covenant with Him.

Today we take for granted that anyone with an interest can acquire and study the scriptures. But for centuries after Jesus walked the earth, made His promises to us in person, and showed us how to obtain His grace and mercy, access to the Bible was limited to a select few—the rulers, the clergy, the learned, and the wealthy. Books were costly to make, and literacy was uncommon. The clergy actively protected their exclusive franchise to sparingly dole out the word of God. More than five hundred years ago, a few men (inspired by God, I believe) began to make the scriptures readable and available to common men and women. John Wycliffe (in England) and Martin Luther (in Germany) were two early pioneers who risked their lives to translate the Bible into the language of the people. William Tyndale, who was burned at the stake for his efforts, strove to make it possible for a plowboy to know more about the scriptures than a priest. By the end of the sixteenth century, multiple common language translations of the Bible were in circulation, including the Great Bible, the Geneva Bible (brought to the New World by the Pilgrims on the *Mayflower*), as well as Tyndale's and Luther's translations.

In 1611, newly crowned King James I of England (James VI of Scotland), concerned that the Geneva Bible questioned kingly and clerical authority, authorized a new English translation. Forty-seven British scholars worked on the project, drawing heavily upon Tyndale's beautiful translation, and produced a version of the Bible that has become the most widely sold book in the history of the world, with an estimated one billion copies printed.

As a witness of the power that reading the scriptures brings, once the English had the King James Version, they could know for themselves what James did not want them to know—that God was not pleased with His people when they demanded the prophet Samuel anoint an earthly king to govern them and that most earthly kings were deficient in righteousness and deserving of punishment. Only a few decades after James I published his version of the Bible, it became the authority for those who opposed the divine right of King Charles (son and heir of James I) to rule, leading to a civil war. After he lost the civil war, King Charles was beheaded, surely an unintended consequence of making the biblical text available in every English home.

Beyond the power to move political consensus, the Bible speaks to its readers about human nature and how to move and motivate the human heart. Jesus, who Christians believe to be the central biblical figure, said, "Lay not up for yourselves treasures upon earth, where moth and rust doth corrupt, and where thieves break through and steal: but lay up for yourselves treasures in heaven, where neither moth nor rust doth corrupt, and where thieves do not break through nor steal: for where your treasure is, there will your heart be also" (Matthew 6:19–21).

The Bible makes it clear that each individual can choose what to treasure. These choices determine what's in our heart and therefore what motivates our thoughts and actions. Biblically speaking, we become what we value, which was quite a radical idea when Moses began to articulate it as he wrote the first five books of the Old Testament:

> And the Lord passed by before [Moses], and proclaimed, The Lord, The Lord God, merciful and gracious, longsuffering, and abundant in goodness and truth keeping mercy for thousands, forgiving iniquity and transgression and sin, and that will by no means clear the guilty. . . . I make a covenant: before all thy people I will do marvels, such as have not been done in all the earth. (Exodus 34:6–10)
>
> Ye have seen . . . how I bare you on eagles' wings, and brought you unto myself. Now therefore, if ye will obey my voice indeed, and keep my covenant, then ye shall be a peculiar treasure unto me above all people: for all the earth is mine: and ye shall be unto me a kingdom of priests, and an holy nation. (Exodus 19:4–6)

It's a startlingly simple formula—if we value what God has to offer, He will make us holy. God cares about our values because He knows what will make us happy and He lives to help us be happy.

Back when King James decreed there would be a new English version of the Bible, there was consensus in England and, for that matter, in the European world from Moscow to Madrid, that what God caused to be written in the Bible, though it was said or written originally in a small area around Jerusalem, applied universally. English Bible readers have made the King James Version the most popular Bible during the four hundred years since it was published, and they have taken it throughout the world of the once-mighty British Empire, which, at its peak, included a mandate to govern in Jerusalem.

In the centuries since the publication of the King James Version, however, mankind has first questioned the meaning of the Bible and then largely decided to live without biblical guidance. Just a few generations ago, the Bible was the principal book in every household, read broadly and understood, if not wholly embraced. Today, few people read the Bible, and fewer still understand it or refer to it. In biblical terms, rather than accept that we are God's "workmanship, created in Christ Jesus unto good works" which God "ordained that we should walk in," we are "without Christ, being aliens from the commonwealth of Israel, and strangers from the covenants of promise, having no hope, and without God in the world" (Ephesians 2:10, 12).

Ironically, some who have led us away from biblical living did so using the Bible itself to dress up their assertions with authority. A prime example of this process of using biblical references to abandon biblical living was the Jesus Seminar, a group of 150 persons founded in 1985 whose stated purpose was to offer a collective view about what Jesus actually said and did as opposed to what is "alleged" in the New Testament. Rooted in modern scholarly methods, the Jesus Seminar approached the text of the Bible as an historical document with nonfactual elaborations alleging divine interventions added by believers to shore up communal faith. By a process of voting, the members of the seminar intended to establish what the mortal man named Jesus actually said and did, having rejected at the outset any notion that prophecy, healing, atonement, and resurrection were even possible. Of course, voting is a questionable method for establishing truth. They relied on the text of the Bible, or at least their critical understanding of it, as well as upon the modern findings of textual analysis, archeology, and history. But because they started from the presumption that Jesus could not be the Only Begotten of the Father in the flesh, that miracles could not happen, and that a Resurrection wasn't possible, they were limited to find only what they had presupposed. This is a classic example of confirmation bias in scholarship.

It is not the purpose of this book to provide a scholarly response to the Jesus Seminar or other biblical minimalists. Rather, this book is a statement of my personal experiences and observations as I have encountered the Bible through reading it, striving to apply its principles, and visiting the ancient places where it was written. I, too, have augmented my study of the Bible by reading history, visiting archeological sites, and applying the methods of science and literature I was taught during college and graduate education. As a lifelong practicing member of The Church of Jesus Christ of Latter-day Saints, I bring skepticism to any encounter with group-think theology, from the Nicene Creed (also an attempt at orthodoxy by vote) to the Jesus Seminar. Truth manifestly is not the preserve of scholars or elites but can be experienced by any human living at any time in history anywhere on the face of the earth. The first step toward discerning truth is to be open to possibilities, to be willing to consider ideas beyond the current limits of your knowledge. When you give both your mind and heart the freedom to search for truth and you do it with real intent (you agree to act on and according to truth as it is revealed to you), God will manifest it to you.

It is truth at that basic level that is the core biblical experience. The Bible is a book of prophecy, promises, covenants, miracles, atonement, and ultimately resurrection. As we read it, we are invited to prevail upon Him to help us with our trials and partake in the blessings God extends to those who keep His commandments. Two hundred years ago, my ancestors were immersed in these biblical ideas, ideas that made them ready for new blessings as they encountered the restored gospel of Jesus Christ and the additions to the scriptural canon revealed by God to Joseph Smith. By striving to become biblically literate, I have endeavored to understand their biblical point of view while living in the postbiblical modern world. Regrettably, in my search for biblical truth and experience, I don't have the advantage my ancestors did living in a society steeped in biblical belief. The one advantage I do have is that in the two hundred years since they encountered the restored gospel of Jesus Christ, many Old Testament prophecies have been fulfilled, adding to my understanding of the promises of God. I know what has happened during the two hundred years since they lived and believed biblically.

From my vantage point in the United States and the twenty-first century, I feel the impact of what Jewish prophets foresaw three millennia ago as Jerusalem, in their view, ripened for destruction. I choose to treasure their wisdom that we are God's workmanship, meant to enjoy fellowship in the house of Israel and to have hope through the covenants of promise. Having walked where Jesus walked in what is now the modern State of Israel (the birthplace of where people first learned to prevail upon God to bless them), this book is my chance to tell you, gentle reader, why I choose to open my heart to what happened in Jerusalem. It remains for me a startling story. My hope is that as you join me on this journey through Israel, visiting the very sites where Jesus walked and taught in His mortal ministry, you will gain your own treasure: a witness that Jesus is our Lord and Redeemer, the God of the Old and the New Testaments, and a testimony that His promises are sure.

For the purpose of this book, the term *monotheism* refers to Judaism, Christianity, and Islam. Abraham is generally considered to be the spiritual founding father of these three religions. Teachings within The Church of Jesus Christ of Latter-day Saints find the roots of Abrahamic monotheism stretching further back. According to these teachings, Abraham restored the monotheistic faith first revealed to Adam and subsequently taught to Enoch, Noah, and other ancient patriarchs.

CHAPTER 1

KING OF THE JEWS

A colossus in the history of the land of Israel, King Herod the Great built much of what is now most memorable about a visit to the Holy Land: Temple Mount, Masada, the Herodium, Herod's Palace in Jerusalem, the pleasure palace in Jericho, and the ruin pictured on page 9, Caesarea Maritima, King Herod's Mediterranean port and Roman city. Matthew, the writer of the first Gospel, claims King Herod was still alive when Jesus was born, and still making trouble, as he was wont to do. Herod received the Wise Men, who came asking about the newborn King of the Jews, and became alarmed—after all, Herod fashioned himself to be king of the Jews, and now nearing the end of his life, he was embroiled in a succession crisis within his own family. He had many ambitious wives and even more ambitious sons, all looking to cash in on their relationship with the second most powerful and wealthy man of the Roman Empire.

Historically, there can be no doubt that King Herod lived, and his character is well known. While there is historical doubt as to whether the slaughter of the innocents actually happened (the killing of babies

The ruins of Herod's Palace at Caesarea Maritima on the Israeli Mediterranean coast

in Bethlehem after the Wise Men failed to return to the palace with a report about the whereabouts of Jesus), there is no doubt King Herod was perfectly capable of ordering such atrocity. According to Josephus, a Jew-turned-Roman historian, upon his deathbed, Herod brought many distinguished men from across his kingdom to Jericho and had them locked up in the hippodrome with orders that they be executed as soon as he died. He apparently reasoned that killing these beloved community leaders would lead many of their followers and family to mourn during the time immediately after his passing, which otherwise would have been a time of great celebration. According to Josephus, the order was not carried out. Jesus, on the other hand, is someone whose historical existence is frequently questioned, particularly the version of Him found in the New Testament. The controversy begins with His birth. If, as Matthew asserts, King Herod was still alive when Mary produced her firstborn, then Jesus was likely born in 4 BC, just before the old king's death. Luke, however, insists the birth occurred when "all the world should be taxed" (Luke 2:1) during the time Cyrenius was the Roman governor of Syria. This taxation event, likely a census, would not have happened while King Herod lived for the simple reason that as king, he had been entrusted by the Romans with collecting taxes however he saw fit. Caesar Augustus would not have gone to the trouble of conducting a census in Judea. He deferred all such matters to Herod, who ruled for Rome in that part of the world. If Luke is correct, the birth of Jesus would have occurred in about 6 AD, or ten years after the time Matthew dates it.

Those who contend that Jesus is not really a historical figure, certainly not the man of miracles and wisdom portrayed in the Gospels, seize on textual problems in the Bible, such as the dating of the birth of Christ, and hold them up as evidence that not much about the Bible can be accepted as fact. These biblical minimalists readily accept King Herod as an historical figure but would have us ignore Jesus, if not completely, then at least insofar as His divine nature is concerned.

In effect, the Bible poses a question to its readers: Who was the real king of the Jews two thousand years ago? Was it Herod the Great, whose physical impact on the Holy Land was immense then and obviously lingers still? Or was it Jesus of Nazareth, who didn't leave an archeological trace on His homeland but has had an indelible impact on the hearts and minds of the billions of His brothers and sisters born since His mortal sojourn in the Galilee and Jerusalem. King Herod and Jesus had an impact on people during their lifetimes. Intentionally using violence to quell disobedience, Herod induced fear in his subjects. Jesus, however, induced "the people [to be] astonished at his doctrine: for he taught them as one having authority" (Matthew 7:28–29). Which kind of king moves you? A king who demands that his people sacrifice their lives and well-being to satisfy his craving for wealth and architecture or a king who astonishes you with his doctrine?

CAESAREA MARITIMA

Caesarea Maritima, King Herod's Roman port and fortified city, lay at the heart of his efforts to remake the Judean economy to please himself.

He intentionally accumulated wealth, carefully managing the sources of income he inherited from his predecessors, such as the massive wealth of the Judean temple and the spice trade. It was his prerogative as king to designate who would be the chief priest in Jerusalem, and he therefore exercised authority over the fiscal affairs of the Hebrew temple, ensuring his own enrichment. To be fair, Herod spent forty years rebuilding the temple and the mount upon which it stood into a glorious edifice of international renown. And some historical sources state that Herod controlled the spice trade routes from the east into the Mediterranean area with tax-collecting fortifications, such as Masada.

More to the point of the New Testament story, however, was how Herod changed the nature of the Judean countryside's economy from subsistence farming (and fishing in the Galilee) to an export business. Fish sauce manufactured in Magdala on the Sea of Galilee was *the* condiment of that Roman era. Fishing boats were heavily taxed, requiring multiple families enterprising together to both pay the taxes and earn a living. Likewise, subsistence family farms were heavily taxed. And when the taxes couldn't be paid, the tax collectors conveniently offered what were, in essence, pay-day loans with exorbitant interest rates, which, of course, eventually drove the families off the farms and left the land to larger agribusiness interests that farmed for export.

Caesarea Maritima was built to be the port through which all of this export business made its way across the Roman Empire, enriching King Herod while at the same time impoverishing the country people of Judea in the Galilee. This is why the miracle of the loaves and fishes was such a sensation. King Herod created the world of want and anguish into which Jesus walked during His ministry. And with his wealth, King Herod built the luxurious palaces he so enjoyed, including the ruined one shown on page 9 with its Mediterranean swimming pool. He also built the public structures so common to Roman cities, such as a hippodrome and theater, pictured on the next page.

Following King Herod's death and the failure of his son to keep the

The ruins of the hippodrome at Caesarea Maritima

The ruins of the Roman theater at Caesarea Maritima

peace in poverty-stricken Judea, Roman prelates were assigned to rule in Jerusalem. They likely would have used Herod's palaces for their own purposes. Roman governor Pontius Pilate did none of the building for which King Herod is famous. His would have been an unremarkable tenure in a backwater of the Roman Empire, perhaps totally unknown to anyone but for the accounts of the trial of Jesus in the New Testament. Because Pilate plays a linchpin role in the Crucifixion/Resurrection story, if he were to prove to be an invented or nonhistorical figure, the origins of Christianity would be in doubt. However, in Caesarea Maritima, where King Herod established his wealth and built his most Roman city, the historicity of both King Herod and Pilate has been established. In 1961, archeologists discovered a stone with the name Pontius Pilate etched in it. The stone can be seen today in the Israel Museum in Jerusalem. So we begin our look into the latter-day Holy Land by visiting King Herod's city, where we find evidence that the Roman who condemned Jesus to death did live there.

King Herod and Pilate are historical figures whose lives frame the mortal life of Jesus. Biblical minimalists, at most, accept Jesus as likewise an historical person but of a pathetic nature. They assert that He taught lofty principles, told insightful parables, and captured the imagination of many followers but died miserably, crucified for defying the political establishment in Jerusalem. When minimalists read the Bible, they preemptively strike any reference to prophecy or miracle from what they accept as truth because they find no evidence for what they call the supernatural in the world of their own experience.

The ruins of an arched entrance to the Roman theater at Caesarea Maritima

The "rose of Sharon" mentioned in the Song of Solomon and found on the coastal plain of Sharon around Caesarea Maritima

Caesarea Maritima was where Pilate's successor, Festus, held the Apostle Paul before sending him to Rome for trial. During Paul's prolonged stay there, Festus received the visit of King Herod's great-grandson Herod Agrippa, who, unlike Festus, was schooled in Jewish prophecy. Paul used the things "the prophets and Moses did say should come: that Christ should suffer, and that he should be the first that should rise from the dead, and should shew light unto the people, and to the Gentile" (Acts 26:22–23), almost convincing Agrippa of the promise of Christianity, which "hope of the promise" (Acts 26:6) Paul characterized with a question: "Why should it be thought a thing incredible with you, that God should raise the dead?" (Acts 26:8).

Our task in this visit to the modern-day Holy Land is to find the hard historical evidences of the existence of biblical figures, or not, and use that framework to understand the "hope of the promise" of ancient scriptural prophecy as it is being fulfilled in the modern land of Israel and in our own lives.

ELIJAH THE PROPHET

A short way up the Mediterranean coast from Caesarea Maritima lies a mountain range not quite two thousand feet high named Mount Carmel, which divides the coastal plain of Sharon from the modern port city of Haifa, pictured on page 15.

Haifa is home to the beautiful Bahai Gardens, as seen on the following page.

Toward the east of Mount Carmel is the Jezreel Valley, also on the following page.

Today, at the top of Mount Carmel, one can find a statue of Elijah (page 17), a prophet who lived nine centuries before King Herod the Great.

Mount Carmel is geographically central to the story of Elijah's life as it is told in the book of 1 Kings in the Old Testament. Elijah, whose name means "Jehovah is my God," was constantly in conflict with King Ahab, ruler of the Northern Kingdom of Israel, and Ahab's queen, Jezebel, who was a Baal worshipper from Phoenicia, to the north.

In this conflict, Elijah's first strategy is to directly attack Baal, the god of harvest, rain, and dew, by calling upon God to cause a drought and famine so severe that not even dew forms. This defiance earns him a death sentence from Jezebel, and he flees for his life to the east, across the Jordan River, to a brook called Chorath in what is now the country of Jordan. There he is fed by ravens and drinks from the brook until it dries up due to

The port of Haifa on the northern Mediterranean coast of Israel

The Bahai Gardens in Haifa, Israel

The Jezreel Valley as seen from Mount Carmel

the drought. God then directs Elijah to hide out, ironically, in Phoenicia, Jezebel's native country, to the north of the kingdom of Israel, in a town called Zarephath, located in modern-day Lebanon.

There, Elijah is received by a widow and her son who are about to make their last meal and then await death from famine. At Elijah's bidding, they faithfully share that final meal with him and are then blessed by the miracle he promises—that their food stores will never dwindle. The son, who by Jewish tradition later grows up to be the prophet Jonah, dies while Elijah is living with the family but is brought back to life by Elijah's intercession with God, the first instance of the raising of the dead recorded in scripture. After three years of drought, God tells Elijah to go back to King Ahab and make an end to the famine. Elijah chooses to end the drought by arranging a contest of the deities on Mount Carmel. Baal and Jehovah are each asked by their separate worshippers to set a meat offering on fire while the children of Israel, now predominantly Baal worshippers, look on.

According to the writer of 1 Kings, only seven thousand Israelites are

The statue of Elijah atop Mount Carmel

still Jehovah worshippers. This rebellion against God has been led by King Ahab, who boasts he has violated every one of the ten commandments yet has every good thing despite the promise of Moses that breaking the commandments leads to punishment. Jewish folklore adds detail to the contest on Mount Carmel: the priests of Baal hide someone underneath their altar who is supposed to start the fire for Baal, but Jehovah sends a poisonous serpent under the altar to kill the kindler and frustrate the pantheists' plans.

Jehovah, the only true and living God, the God of Abraham, Isaac, and Jacob, prevails in this contest, for "the fire of the Lord [falls], and [consumes] the burnt sacrifice, and the wood, and the stones, and the dust, and [licks] up [the twelve barrels of] water" Elijah has caused to be poured on the meat sacrifice. (Elijah is making it impossible for any witness to deny that what has occurred is a divine miracle.) Then Elijah executes the 450 priests of Baal and causes a great rain to end the drought while the people acknowledge, "The Lord, he is the God." (Readers often make the mistake of interpreting actions in the scriptures through modern prejudices, but the reality is that Elijah understood that the worship of Baal, which included religious prostitution and the barbaric act of child sacrifice, was so vile it could not be allowed to take root again. This was a battle for the heart and soul of Israel and her people. To leave the prophets of Baal alive would have been to allow the cancer to continue to grow.)

If Elijah thought this demonstration of God's power would put an end to Baal worship, he was sorely disappointed. In fact, because of the killing of the priests of Baal, Jezebel again put a price on Elijah's head, and he was once more forced to flee, this time south to Beersheba and from there to the Sinai Peninsula (in modern-day Egypt) and Mount Horeb, the mountain of God where Moses received the ten commandments. Elijah journeyed in all directions of the compass during his ministry in Israel, covering territory north to south from modern-day Lebanon to Egypt, and east to west from Syria and Jordan to the coast of Israel, but failed to achieve his desire to bring the people of Israel back to their God.

Obviously, the biblical minimalist rejects the entire story of Elijah. We have nothing in the archeological record to document his life. He was not a builder like King Herod, leaving structural remnants for us to visit. He did not even write a book of prophecy for us to read, like the later prophets of Israel, such as Isaiah. But for those who choose to believe, he left ancient promises to seek and embrace.

In his hour of travail, after he believes himself a failure and prays, "It is enough; now, O Lord, take away my life; for I am not better than my fathers" (1 Kings 19:4), he is fed and nourished by God and led to His mount, where he is touched by the still, small voice (see 1 Kings 19:12), refreshed, and sent on his final mission. We, too, are promised that faithful service, even if frustrated by events outside our control, will be blessed by spiritual gifts often known only to us. Biblical minimalists, keen on reviewing evidence, never experience the evidence of the still, small voice.

ELIJAH'S MISSION

The final event of Elijah's mortal life brings an even greater ancient promise, one that still enthralls Jews today. Elijah is taken to heaven without tasting death, in full view of Elisha, his successor, who receives the prophet's mantle as Elijah ascends. Jews believe Elijah is held in heaven for a special mission on earth: protector of the innocent, inspiration of hope and confidence in the downtrodden, and helper of the poor. He is the stern avenger of wrong. He constrains people to be humble. He is a great teacher, providing insight into the deep meanings of the scriptures. He helps people understand the meaning of suffering—how God is just despite the pain and suffering of mortality. He is the forerunner of the Messiah and, as such, will restore the twelve tribes, persuade Israel to repent, and bring peace and harmony to the world. In the end, he will blow the trumpet that brings the dead back to life and restores the temple in Jerusalem.

Members of The Church of Jesus Christ of Latter-day Saints find a more specific assignment for Elijah in his translated state. As promised in all four books of scripture we hold sacred, God has said, "I will reveal unto you the priesthood, by the hand of Elijah the prophet, before the coming of the great and dreadful day of the Lord. And he shall plant in the hearts of the children the promises made to the fathers, and the hearts of the children shall turn to their fathers. If it were not so, the whole earth would be utterly wasted at his coming" (D&C 2:1–3).

It is through Elijah that we are promised the full blessing of the priesthood, which promise has been fulfilled (see D&C 110). Through the revelation of the priesthood brought about by the faithfulness of Elijah, the greatest prophet between Moses and Jesus Christ, we are endowed with the sealing power, allowing us to minister to God's children here on earth, both those present now and all who have ever lived, by eternally uniting husbands and wives, children and parents. While Elijah may yet have other work to do on earth before the Second Coming of Christ, by his bringing to us this sacred priesthood power, we have become the hands of God throughout the world ascribed by Jewish tradition to the prophet Elijah himself, helping to serve others in whatever ways we can, comforting those who stand in need of comfort, lifting the downtrodden, and standing as witnesses of Christ in all things (see Mosiah 18:9).

As Elijah is translated, he promises his successor, Elisha, a double portion of the Spirit of God to assist him with the work of ministry that now falls to him. Like Elisha, let us take the mantle of ministry which falls to us, strike the barriers in our way, and ask, "Where is the Lord God of Elijah?" (2 Kings 2:14), meaning that we, like Elisha, expect God to support and empower us in our righteous quests, just as He did Elijah.

ABRAHAM THE PATRIARCH

In the northeast corner of the modern State of Israel where the borders of Lebanon, Syria, and Israel meet at the culmination of the Golan Heights is a mountainous region commonly called Mount Hermon. The tallest peak is over

The heights of Mount Hermon shrouded in cloud

nine thousand feet and boasts a ski resort (page 22). Pictured on page 23 is a secondary peak in the Mount Hermon complex called Har Habtarim. According to Jewish tradition, this is where Abraham received the covenant with God upon his arrival in the land of Canaan, his new home.

The view from near the top of Mount Hermon in the spring

The journey that brought Abraham to Mount Hermon is recorded in Genesis of the Old Testament, with significant additional details found in the book of Abraham in the Pearl of Great Price (part of the canon of scripture accepted by members of The Church of Jesus Christ of Latter-day Saints). According to scripture, Abraham lived in Ur, a city in Mesopotamia (located in what is now Iraq). He was a man who sought to preserve the teachings of righteousness

A ski lift on Mount Hermon

handed down by his ancestors but was opposed by those who had become followers of a perverted and pantheistic religion. Abraham described this counterfeit religion, or belief system, as the worship of dumb idols involving the sacrifice of human life, including children and young virgins.

Biblical minimalists insist that no person named Abraham ever existed, certainly not as he is described in the Bible, which is as a friend of God. The lack of archeological evidence for Abraham is understandable because he was a nomad who never

A Druze village, Majdal Shams, high on the slopes of Mount Hermon

built a structure other than tents. There is plenty of archeological evidence, however, that religious practices in Mesopotamia, the cradle of human civilization where the beginnings of writing and the earliest known cities have been documented, would have involved the worship of idols with human sacrifice nearly four thousand years ago, when Abraham is thought to have lived.

The worldview of idol worshippers in Mesopotamia four thousand years ago can be summed as a belief that life is cyclical: everything revolves around eternally recurring patterns so that nothing new or different ever happens. Mesopotamians' expectations of life would have been that sameness prevailed and that variability didn't occur; what had happened before would happen again. In this worldview, there was no sense of history and therefore no sense in striving. There were no choices for individuals whose moments were determined by the fate assigned them. People could view the heavens and see the heavenly bodies, who were identified as deities. They could project drama onto these heavenly entities and believed those

Har Habtarim, a peak in the Mount Hermon mountain range, where, according to Jewish tradition, Abraham received the covenant

entities could perhaps be appeased by sacrifice. But, ultimately, the heavens were unreachable by humans no matter how high one built a sacrificial edifice. The only option and the course encouraged by polytheism and mythology, just like the practices of superstition and atheism today, was to resign oneself to fate, even if that meant dying on an altar. What happened to you didn't really matter after all.

Abraham just didn't believe any of that. Rather than accept his fate as a sacrificial victim, Abraham reached out to the God he had been taught to believe in. And God responded: "Behold, I will lead thee by my hand, and I will take thee, to put upon thee my name . . . and my power shall be over thee. . . . through thy ministry my name shall be known in the earth forever, for I am thy God" (Abraham 1:18–19). And with that conversation, the first of many between God and men associated with monotheism, God and Abraham forever changed the history of mankind.

It has been said that monotheism is the only new idea human beings have ever had. Better said, it is the principal new idea revealed to man by God. Because he reached out to have a relationship of love with God, Abraham chose to follow God's directions and make a long journey to a strange land, which ended at Har Habtarim, where the relationship between God and man was memorialized forever as a covenant. The essence of this covenant is that men and women need not passively accept fate. Rather, through covenant, God promises each of His children He will help them make history by offering them choices. In fact, Abraham's whole life opened up with the choices he could make. Rather than accept fate, Abraham learned to live in the present, where his choices were written into a consequential personal history, a history that mattered because friendship with God proved that God thought that what Abraham, and, by extension, the rest of mankind, did made a difference. What Elijah was fighting on Mount Carmel was the continual backsliding of mankind from embracing the Abrahamic covenant with its life of consequence into the easy, passive, superstitious, and inconsequential lives of materialism, pantheism, or atheism. That alternative has always been the chief rival of faith, which is love of God.

Monotheism—with its emphasis on the merits of individual choice and personal striving to make eternal history—has blessed humanity since Abraham. No wonder Abraham is honored by the three major mono-theistic traditions associated with the Middle East: Judaism, Christianity, and Islam. Abraham and his son and grandson patriarchs, Isaac and Jacob, who followed his covenant are honored in several places in Israel. At Hebron, pictured right, is found the tomb of the patriarchs and matriarchs.

The Tomb of the Patriarchs and Matriarchs in Hebron, Israel

Mount Moriah, now known as

The Abrahamic Gate at Tel Dan

Spring water near Tel Dan, which forms part of the origins of the Jordan River

Temple Mount in Jerusalem, is the biblical scene of the would-be sacrifice of Isaac, an episode that best illustrates the potentially fearful presence of God in our lives under the Abrahamic covenant. This story asks us if we can be open to God in our lives, whatever He asks of us. Finally, there is the Abrahamic Gate at Tel Dan, at the foot of Mount Hermon in Northern Israel, pictured on page 25.

The tribe of Dan was originally settled by Joshua along the Mediterranean coast. But they found the presence of Philistines in that neighborhood to be a deterrent to their prosperity and asked to be relocated. They moved north to the foothills of Mount Hermon and built a city called Dan, which is often referenced as the northernmost settlement of the twelve tribes. The people of Dan believed Abraham rescued Lot from captivity (see Genesis 14) somewhere in the neighborhood of their city. Thus, they gave the main gate of their city the name of their patriarchal ancestor.

The snows that fall on Mount Hermon are the source of the Jordan

The ruin of a temple at Tel Dan

The ruins of Caesarea Philippi and its shrine to the god Pan

Spring water at Caesarea Philippi, part of the origins of the Jordan River

River, the fresh mountain runoff emerging at the base of the mountain in multiple springs where ancient cities, including Dan, were established to take advantage of this water source.

Caesarea Philippi

Another ancient city located at a well source for the Jordan River was known as Caesarea Philippi during the time of Jesus (pictured on page 28).

By the time of Christ, this city had been fashioned into a center of Hellenistic pagan worship of the deity Pan and was ruled by the Herodian kings. What can be seen of the ruin of this Greco-Roman-Herodian city is mostly the remnant of the etchings to Pan inscribed over the grotto from which emerged the then much larger spring of water. The flow of water today lies a short distance from where it now seeps out of the rocks (see page 28).

The Jordan River downstream from the ruins of Caesarea Philippi

CHAPTER 2

THE SAVIOR'S OBSERVATION OF THE FEASTS

Jesus was raised by His earthly parents to be an observant Jew and remained so His entire life. This is evident in the stories preserved about Him in the Gospels. He consistently observed the Sabbath and participated in synagogue services, going out of His way to fulfill an assignment to read from the scriptures to His hometown congregation in Nazareth. In the Gospel stories, we frequently find Jesus teaching and healing at synagogue on the Sabbath. Likewise, throughout His life, He honored and observed temple practices in Jerusalem. His parents presented Him in the temple after Mary's ritual postpartum purification as prescribed in the Torah for the redemption of the firstborn son. Luke informs us that Mary and Joseph went to Jerusalem every year at the Feast of the Passover, the first of the three annual temple or sanctuary feast seasons required of Israel by God in the law of Moses. It was when Jesus was twelve years old and in Jerusalem for the Passover that He remained at the temple in dialogue with scholars, requiring His parents to turn back on their way to Nazareth to look for Him. During His three-year ministry, Jesus continued to honor these sanctuary feast seasons, returning repeatedly to Jerusalem and the temple. And He was no shrinking violet on these occasions. Twice, He cleansed the courts of the temple, often confronting the Pharisees, such as when He defended the woman taken in adultery.

In keeping these sanctuary feasts, Jesus was obeying the law of Moses as summarized in Leviticus 23, which lists eight feasts Israel was to observe: 1) the Sabbath, celebrated weekly; 2) the feasts of the Passover, Unleavened Bread, and Firstfruits, celebrated every spring; 3) the Feast of Weeks, or Pentecost, celebrated in the summer; 4) and the Feasts of Trumpets, Atonement, and Tabernacles, celebrated in the fall. The Lord's promise to Israel if they kept the law of Moses was: "I will give you rain in due season. . . . And I will give peace in the land. . . . For I will have respect unto you, and make you fruitful, and multiply you, and establish my covenant with you. . . . And I will set my tabernacle among you: and my soul shall not abhor you. And I will walk among you, and will be your God, and ye shall be my people" (Leviticus 26:4–12).

Jesus was the Jehovah of the Old Testament who promised He would walk among Israel and be their God. While He was physically doing exactly that, He did not fail to follow His own commandments to Israel; He religiously kept the sanctuary feasts.

So, it would have been a great surprise to His close-knit group of followers, the Apostles, that as the fall festivals approached one year, rather than head south from Galilee toward Jerusalem, Jesus led them north and uphill toward the source of the Jordan River in the foothills of Mount Hermon. Jesus would have known He was missing the last Feast of Tabernacles to occur while He lived on the earth, but the Apostles were unaware. While all Israel was celebrating the Feasts of Trumpets and Atonement in Jerusalem, the holiest days of the Jewish calendar, Jesus and His brethren were staying in Caesarea Philippi, a pagan city not founded nor ever lived in by Jews.

Those who visit the ruins of Caesarea Philippi today can still see the stream of spring water, one of three major springs feeding the Jordan River, emerging from the mountainside. In the Savior's time, the flow of water was apparently much greater than today's modest creek. Also visible are the remnants of pagan worship of the Greek god Pan. The Greeks under Alexander the Great had been the first to create a city to take advantage of the massive flow of spring water there. Because Pan is the god of the wilderness, he was most commonly worshipped with not a structure or temple but with carvings on mountain walls near grottos, such as the one located at Caesarea Philippi. It is no small irony that Pan is the only Greek god to have ever been alleged to die; his death has been viewed as the harbinger of the demise of paganism as it gave way to Christianity as the dominant religion of the Roman Empire.

I believe Jesus brought the Apostles to the shrine of Pan in order to give context to what He wanted to teach them. Pan, representative of all paganism, was everything Jehovah had fiercely opposed while revealing His will to His people Israel. Paganism, like all forms of belief other than monotheism, including the versions of superstition and atheism prevalent today, teaches the children of God that they can make no significant difference in this life. By insisting that life cycles on endlessly as directed by a pantheon of mythical deities, or by chance alone, or physical forces and matter spontaneously combining, paganism, superstition, or atheism induce a moral torpor upon humankind. Why act, or even try to understand the human condition, if what we do or say or think changes nothing? The heavens are beyond our reach, so we might as well give in to "natural" urges, for we all are hurtling irresistibly on to a personal oblivion.

As Jehovah, Jesus had repeatedly warned Israel that you only lost control of your destiny when you let go of the hand of God. Elijah, who lived and prophesied when only a handful of Israelites still followed Jehovah, stated the problem forcefully: "How long halt ye between two opinions? If the Lord be God, follow him: but if Baal, then follow him. And the people answered him not a word" (1 Kings 18:21). Jesus took His Apostles to the equivalent of a Baal shrine of His own era to ask them a similar question:

"When Jesus came into the coasts of Caesarea Philippi, he asked his disciples, saying: Whom do men say that I the Son of man am? And they said, Some say that thou art John the Baptist; some, Elias; and others, Jeremias, or one of the prophets. He saith unto them, but whom say ye that I am? And Simon Peter answered and said, Thou art the Christ, the Son of the living God" (Matthew 16:13–16).

Jesus then declared that Peter had received this truth from God and that revelation like this would be the rock upon which Christ's Church would be built. He also promised Peter that he would receive the necessary keys to lead the Church.

"From that time forth began Jesus to shew unto his disciples, how that he must go unto Jerusalem, and suffer many things of the elders and chief priests and scribes, and be killed, and be raised again the third day" (Matthew 16:21). Right there, in front of a shrine to paganism, just at the time when all Israel was at the temple for the festivities of the Feasts of Trumpets and Atonement and about six months before His Crucifixion, Jesus began to teach His closest associates what it meant to be the promised Messiah. That this teaching was hard for them to understand is, of course, clear from Matthew's record.

FEASTS OF TRUMPETS AND ATONEMENT

What occurs at the Feasts of Trumpets and Atonement should have helped the Apostles understand what Jesus taught about His role as Messiah. The Feast of Trumpets is the Jewish New Year, or Rosh Hashanah. The trumpets or shofars were blown to wake Israel up and remind them who they really were: the children of God, not insignificant pawns in an uncaring universe. Rosh Hashanah, according to Jewish tradition, marks the sixth day of creation, the day Adam and Eve were created. The blast of the trumpets also begins the ten days of awe, of taking stock of one's life, and of confessing one's sins, which ends on Yom Kippur, the feast day of atonement, the holiest day in the Jewish annual calendar. This is the day of deliverance and salvation, and according to Jewish tradition, it is the day Moses returned from Mount Sinai with the second set of tablets, his face shining because he had met Jehovah face-to-face. Yom Kippur is the one day each year when the high priest, representing all of Israel like Moses when meeting God on Mount Sinai, entered the Holy of Holies in the temple. There he would sprinkle the blood of a bull upon the mercy seat, followed by the sacrifice and spilling the blood of one of two goats. Upon the head of the second goat, the high priest would lay his hands and confess all the sins of the people of Israel. This second goat, the scapegoat, was then driven into the desert. These were, of course, rituals meant to teach the people about the Atonement for their sins, which the coming Messiah would accomplish.

During this time, Jesus was focused on teaching His inner circle of brethren these principles of repentance, sacrifice, and salvation, which would become possible upon the culmination of His atoning sacrifice. As He continued to teach them, they left Caesarea Philippi and began climbing Mount Hermon. They were heading for Har Habtarim, the traditional site where Abraham received the covenant from Jehovah just after he arrived in the land of Canaan. This is the place where Abraham fully separated himself from the pagan traditions of his time, including the human sacrifice that had nearly cost him his life, and embraced monotheism, which through him has blessed every part of the human family since. Abraham, the father of monotheism, established forever the principle that what each child of God does is important, not just to us but to God. Abraham, who became a friend to God, showed all of us how to be in fellowship with the Almighty.

THE FEAST OF TABERNACLES

As Jesus and His small group of travelers made the climb toward Har Habtarim, the Feast of Tabernacles was being celebrated back in Jerusalem.

This festival is the most joyous on the Jewish calendar because it celebrates the renewed fellowship with God Israel enjoyed as they traveled in the wilderness protected, fed, and led by Him. God's presence among His people was guaranteed as they ended their long journey by establishing a tabernacle at Shiloh, followed later by the building of the temple in Jerusalem, which was dedicated by Solomon during the Feast of Tabernacles. The rejoicing during the Feast of Tabernacles is a recognition of the goodness of God in providing an atonement for sin through His presence in Israel. That this Atonement was to exact a price from Jesus was the hard lesson He was trying to teach His Apostles.

Once the group arrived at Har Habtarim, Jesus took three of the Apostles—Peter, James, and John—to the summit. There, a marvelous and joyous event took place: "Jesus was transfigured before them: and his face did shine as the sun, and his raiment was white as the light. And, behold, there appeared unto them Moses and Elias talking with him. Then answered Peter, and said unto Jesus, Lord, it is good for us to be here: if thou wilt, let us make here three tabernacles; one for thee, and one for Moses, and one for Elias" (Matthew 17:2–4).

Peter was referring to the biblical commandment to build temporary shelters for the days of the Feast of Tabernacles to commemorate the goodness of God in providing food, water, shelter, and leadership to Israel throughout their forty years in the wilderness. The three Apostles could now see that Jesus was preeminent over Moses and Elijah, the two predominant prophetic figures of the Old Testament. They could not now doubt that Jesus was Jehovah in the flesh, the God of the Old Testament who had provided the law revealed by Moses, the sealing power, and still, small voice revealed by Elijah. During this pivotal event, these three Apostles received the keys of the kingdom they would need to lead the Church of Jesus Christ after the ascension of the Savior. Jesus was using the limited time He had remaining before the Crucifixion to prepare His Apostles for their coming responsibilities.

During the ensuing months between the Feasts of Tabernacles and

Passover, Jesus returned often to the theme of His coming Crucifixion: "From that time forth began Jesus to shew unto his disciples, how that he must go unto Jerusalem, and suffer many things of the elders and chief priests and scribes, and be killed, and be raised again the third day. Then Peter took him, and began to rebuke him, saying, Be it far from thee, Lord: this shall not be unto thee. But he turned, and said unto Peter, Get thee behind me, Satan: thou art an offence unto me: for thou savourest not the things that be of God, but those that be of men. Then said Jesus unto his disciples, If any man will come after me, let him deny himself, and take up his cross, and follow me. For whosoever will save his life shall lose it: and whosoever will lose his life for my sake shall find it. For what is a man profited, if he shall gain the whole world, and lose his own soul? Or what shall a man give in exchange for his soul?" (Matthew 16:21–26).

He repeated this teaching in the Galilee: "The son of Man shall be betrayed into the hands of men: and they shall kill him, and the third day he shall be raised again. And they were exceeding sorry" (Matthew 17:22–23).

THE FEAST OF THE PASSOVER

Once they were on the way to Jerusalem to attend the Feast of the Passover, He taught this principle again: "And Jesus going up to Jerusalem took the twelve disciples apart in the way, and said unto them, Behold, we go up to Jerusalem; and the Son of man shall be betrayed unto the chief priests and unto the scribes, and they shall condemn him to death, and shall deliver him to the Gentiles to mock, and to scourge, and to crucify him: and the third day he shall rise again" (Matthew 20:17–19).

Jesus was again using the temple festivals to teach the Apostles the principles of everlasting life. They knew they were following their master to Jerusalem to partake of the spring feasts of Passover, unleavened bread, and firstfruits. Once they were near the city, Jesus gave instruction about how the Passover Feast was to be prepared for His small group of followers.

These observant Jewish men knew that Passover celebrated the salvation of Israel at the time of their liberation from slavery in Egypt. This salvation was brought about by the blood of an unblemished lamb sacrificed for each family, the blood of that lamb smeared on their doorposts.

Jesus was identified by John the Baptist as "the Lamb of God, which taketh away the sins of the world" (John 1:29). It was His blood that was about to be spilled because He was "a lamb without blemish and without spot" (1 Peter 1:19). And "then came the day of unleavened bread, when the Passover must be killed. And He sent Peter and John, saying, Go and prepare us the Passover that we may eat. . . . And when the hour was come, He sat down, and the twelve apostles with him. And He said unto them, With desire I have desired to eat this Passover with you before I suffer" (Luke 22:7–15). Jesus was teaching the Apostles the rudiments of being the Messiah right up until He was arrested, which happened precisely at the time of night when Israel originally smeared the blood of the lamb on their doorposts.

The symbolism of the spring feast is enhanced by the reference Luke makes to the Feast of Unleavened Bread, which is the week following the Passover Feast. Being forewarned by Moses, the Israelites prepared unleavened bread the night before God was going to free them from bondage to Egypt. Unleavened bread can be baked without having to wait for the dough to rise. But leaven came to have a deeper meaning for the Israelites as they were commanded by God to remember their liberation. Unleavened bread was often called "the bread of affliction," meaning the bread made while they were waiting to be delivered from affliction or slavery. Removing the leaven came to be seen as a purifying step for the bread and therefore for the person who consumed it.

The Apostle Paul explains this symbolism: "Purge out therefore the old leaven, that ye may be a new lump, as ye are unleavened. For even Christ our Passover is sacrificed for us: therefore let us keep the feast, not with old leaven, neither with the leaven of malice and wickedness; but with the unleavened bread of sincerity and truth" (1 Corinthians 5:7–8).

To this day, orthodox Jews celebrate the Feast of Unleavened Bread by ridding their houses of all leavening, searching every room for this symbol of personal corruption. Jesus specifically mentions the leaven of the Pharisees, which he calls out as hypocrisy (see Luke 12:1). Jesus died on the cross on the first day of the Feast of Unleavened Bread, offering up His body, which was sinless, or symbolically free of leaven. We are to remember this sacrifice every week as we follow the pattern He set for us and partake of the sacramental bread, which represents Him, the bread of life.

THE FEAST OF FIRSTFRUITS

The Feast of Firstfruits, the final spring festival, was held the day after the Sabbath following the Passover. On this day, the Lord required Israel to present a sheaf of spring grain representing the early harvest as a wave offering at the temple. The wave offering was the first grain that rose in the spring, and its purpose was to remind people that God was the source of all their food.

The day after the Jewish Sabbath, of course, was Sunday. The first Easter Sunday, the day Jesus overcame death and became the first of God's children to be resurrected physically and forever, was the festival day of firstfruits in Jerusalem. Again, it is the Apostle Paul who connects the symbolism for us: "But now is Christ risen from the dead, and become the firstfruits of them that slept. For since by man came death, by man came also the resurrection of the dead. For as in Adam all die, even so in Christ shall all be made alive. But every man in his own order: Christ the firstfruits; afterward they that are Christ's at his coming" (1 Corinthians 15:20–23).

The Feast of Firstfruits was the beginning of the seven-week period leading to the summer temple festival in ancient Israel known as the Feast of Weeks, or Pentecost. By Jewish tradition, it was seven weeks after the liberation of Israel when Moses brought the people to Mount Sinai—where he had received his commission from God to go to Egypt and lead Israel to freedom. The Lord then spoke to all Israel: "Ye have seen what I did unto the Egyptians, and how I bare you on eagles' wings, and brought you unto myself. Now therefore, if ye will obey my voice indeed, and keep my covenant, then ye shall be a peculiar treasure unto me above all people: for all the earth is mine. And ye shall be unto me a kingdom of priests, and an holy nation" (Exodus 19:4–6). The Feast of Weeks is a celebration of this covenant relationship between God and His people, which relationship is sustained by the giving of scripture and of the Spirit of the Lord.

DAY OF PENTECOST

After His Resurrection, Jesus sent the Apostles from Jerusalem back to their home territory of the Galilee, where He spent forty days with them. As this time came to an end, He and the Apostles returned to Jerusalem where, just before the time of the Festival of Weeks, or Pentecost, Jesus climbed the Mount of Olives above the Garden of Gethsemane and ascended to heaven after promising that His followers would enjoy the blessing of the Holy Ghost, or Comforter. "And when the day of Pentecost was fully come, they were all with one accord in one place. And suddenly there came a sound from heaven as of a rushing mighty wind, and it filled all the house where they were sitting. And there appeared unto them cloven tongues like as of fire, and it sat upon each of them. And they were all filled with the Holy ghost, and began to speak with other tongues, as the Spirit gave them utterance."

Peter lifted up his voice and said, "This is that which was spoken by the prophet Joel: and it shall come to pass in the last days, saith God, I will pour out of my Spirit upon all flesh: and your sons and your daughters shall prophesy, and your young men shall see visions, and your old men shall dream dreams: and on my servants and on my handmaidens I will pour out in those days of my Spirit: and they shall prophesy" (Acts 2:1–18).

EASTER

Easter is the time each year when we should commemorate how Jesus taught His disciples the truths about the Atonement and Resurrection using the symbolism of the mosaic sanctuary or temple feasts. Easter is the day of the Feast of Firstfruits, when Jesus arose and served as a wave offering to the entire world that life is everlasting. Good Friday is the first day of the Feast of Unleavened Bread, when Jesus, who called Himself the bread of life, offered His sinless body as unleavened bread, the bread of affliction, so that we could remove sin from our lives. Jesus's last meal as a mortal was the Passover Feast, celebrating the salvation of Israel from the destroying angel for those who smeared the blood of an unblemished lamb on their doorposts. Jesus is the Lamb of God, without blemish, whose blood was spilled for us. We are to remember both His body and His blood each week as we partake of His sacrament, which He instituted for us before His passion and which has taken the place of the mosaic temple rituals.

These feasts and observances remind us that we should continually seek fellowship with God, like Abraham on Mount Hermon and Moses and Elijah on Mount Sinai. What we do in this life matters, both to us and to God, who is our Father in Heaven. Jesus explicitly taught His disciples, and through the Gospels they wrote, us, about the joyous nature of the feasts of trumpets, atonement, and tabernacles. He desires us to awake to our true nature as children of God, a peculiar people, a nation of priests, for whom God provides breath and life and guidance so that we can live with joy and purpose.

And finally, let us use the tools revealed to Christians at Pentecost, the sanctuary feast of summer. In mosaic law, this celebrated the giving of the Torah, or law of God, so that mankind could have the commandments of God always before their eyes. In Christian history, Pentecost celebrates the fulfillment of the Savior's promise to provide a Comforter, the Holy Ghost, who brings all good things to our remembrance, expands our capacity for endurance and performance, and quickens us so we can lengthen our stride in God's service.

If we commit to God by observing His laws and commandments, Jehovah's promises to Israel will be ours: He will bear us on eagles' wings and bring us unto Himself. He will give us peace and have respect for us. He will establish His covenant with us and set His tabernacle among us. He will walk among us and be our God, and we shall be His people (see Leviticus 26:4–12).

CHAPTER 3

THE SAVIOR'S
MORTAL MINISTRY

I've seen the Sea of Galilee at sunrise and sunset on many occasions. There, the sun rises over the Golan Heights, which form the eastern boundary of the Galilee, the principal region of Jesus's three-year ministry. To the north of the Galilee is Mount Hermon. The Jordan River rises from springs emerging in the foothills of Mount Hermon and descends to about seven hundred feet below sea level before widening and deepening into the freshwater lake that is the Sea of Galilee. Most of the region named after this body of water extends to its west.

According to the Bible, Jesus grew up in Nazareth and would therefore be a native of the Galilee.

During the time Jesus was a youth, Nazareth was a few miles from Sepphoris, the city called the "Jewel or Ornament of the Galilee." The son of Herod the Great, Herod Antipas, who inherited the Galilee as his administrative district after the death of his father, chose Sepphoris as

Sunset over the Sea of Galilee, looking west toward the territory known as the Galilee

Sunrise over the Sea of Galilee, looking east toward the Golan Heights from Tiberius

The Sea of Galilee as seen from near the city of Tiberius

The modern, mostly Palestinian, city of Nazareth

his capital and invested in rebuilding the city. Herod Antipas is the king who executed John the Baptist and, because of that, the king with whom Jesus would not speak during His trial when Pontius Pilate sent Him to appear before the "king of the Jews."

Sepphoris is not mentioned in the New Testament chronicles of the life of Jesus. Nevertheless, a Christian tradition has developed that has Sepphoris as the birthplace of Mary, the mother of Christ. But a compelling argument can be made that Jesus and His earthly father, Joseph, would have likely found gainful employment in Sepphoris during the expansion and beautification of this capital city by Herod Antipas. Where else would a carpenter or builder like Joseph have found better-paying work in

The Sea of Galilee at sunrise with the Golan Heights in the background

The area around the ruins of Sepphoris arrayed in spring splendor

A mosaic in Sepphoris known as the Mona Lisa of the Galilee

the Galilee than in the region's capital city as it underwent renovation? I believe that when you walk the two-thousand-year-old Roman-era streets in the ruins of Sepphoris, you are walking on pavement Jesus traveled in His youth and early adulthood. Biblical minimalists might agree with that but would probably ask why anyone should care. For those open to the amazing possibility that the Lord of all creation condescended to take upon Himself the pains and afflictions of mortality that He might know intimately how to succor His people, it is truly sacred to walk for a moment where Jesus walked. Though we can come to know Him without visiting the land of His birth, there is an added sense of closeness to the Savior that permeates these historic locations.

The grandeur of Sepphoris can be surmised by examining the ruins of the city today, though the mosaics now seen are from a period later than the Herodians.

Roman era ruts in first-century-AD streets of Sepphoris, where it is likely the youth named Jesus of Nazareth walked and worked

Magdala

In the time of Jesus, the town of Magdala was situated on the west side of the Sea of Galilee. All four Gospels mention the name of this ancient town's most famous resident, Mary Magdalene, who was evidently a close associate of the Savior. Biblical minimalists, were they to express any opinion at all about her, would likely discount her historicity. After all, two Gospel writers would have us believe that Jesus saved her from demonic possession. And she is allegedly a first-person witness to both the Crucifixion and Resurrection. The tender scene between Mary Magdalene and Jesus at the Garden Tomb where she recognizes the Savior by His voice and goes to embrace Him, causing Him to gently remind her that she must let Him go because He must yet appear in resurrected form to His Father in Heaven, has given some, including a few nineteenth-century LDS leaders, cause to believe that Jesus and Mary Magdalene were a married couple. This speculation goes on to assume that the marriage in the Galilean town of Cana, set in time at the start of the Savior's ministry and including the first recorded miracle of the Savior of changing water into wine was the nuptial event for this couple. After all, why would Mary, the mother of Jesus, be concerned about whether enough wine was available to serve guests at the wedding supper unless it was her Son getting married? It must be noted that The Church of Jesus Christ of Latter-day Saints has never offered a doctrinal statement about whether Jesus was married, much less to whom.

Whatever status Mary Magdalene achieved during her earthly life, the ruins of her hometown today are the location of one of the oldest discovered synagogues anywhere, dating to the time Christ would have participated in Galilean Sabbath services. Standing in the ruins of this synagogue, it is not hard to imagine that Jesus might have participated in Sabbath services here on more than one occasion. One can see the remnants of stone benches built against the walls, which appear to have been decorated with elaborately designed, colored frescos. The floor was probably partially made

The floor of the ruin of the first-century AD synagogue in Magdala with a replica of the Torah box discovered therein

Archeological excavation in the ruin of the first-century-AD town of Magdala

of mosaics. A carved stone relief discovered in the synagogue ruins shows a seven-branched menorah flanked by a pair of two-handled jugs and a pair of columns. This is the first menorah to be discovered that dates to the second temple period (516 BC to 70 AD).

The refinements found in this synagogue indicate the wealth and significance of Magdala during the first century AD, when it was the center of the fishing industry on the shores of the Sea of Galilee. Today, nearby, one can see the remains of a first-century fishing boat, the so-called "Jesus Boat." In boats like these, Galilean fishermen, like brothers Peter and Andrew, and their good friends John and James, the sons of Zebedee, plied their craft, probably selling their catch to the fish-sauce processing plants located in Magdala. Perhaps it was a boat like this that served the Savior and His close associates as they traveled from town to town on the coasts of the Sea of Galilee, though I'm sure biblical minimalists would rule out any miraculous stilling of storms or walking on waters.

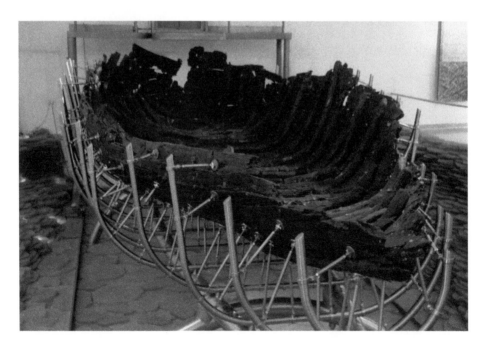

The so-called "Jesus Boat"—a relic fishing boat dated to the first century AD found in the Sea of Galilee

Modern fishermen on the Sea of Galilee

To this day, there are fishers on the Sea of Galilee, although the trade is much diminished. Fish sauce is no longer manufactured. Any fish caught are likely consumed by tourists having a "St. Peter's fish" lunch on the shores of the lake. The modern State of Israel is threatened with water shortages with the Sea of Galilee, a principal source of fresh water, now reduced in size by drought. Even though droughts come and go, there is a source of living water that never ceases to flow. Jesus proclaimed that whoever believes in Him will never thirst. His promises are sure. When we put our trust in Him, we can be assured He is watching out for us both spiritually and temporally.

SABBATH WORSHIP

Jewish Sabbath worship in synagogues, such as the one uncovered in the ruins of Magdala along the shores of the Sea of Galilee, likely began after the fall of Jerusalem and the destruction of the first temple around 586 BC. During the Babylonian captivity and under the leadership of the prophet Ezekiel, those who were in captivity were taught that their sins, including failure to honor the Sabbath day, had weakened them and removed the protection of God from their homeland. Said Ezekiel, "The children [of Israel] rebelled against [God]: they walked not in [His] statutes, neither kept [His] judgments to do them . . . they polluted [the] sabbaths . . . [so God] would pour out [His] fury upon them" (Ezekiel 20:21). Ezekiel taught them to "hallow [His] sabbaths; and they shall be a sign between [God and His people]" (20:20).

Chastened, the Jewish people began to gather together on the Sabbath to remember the covenant they had made with Jehovah and which they hoped to renew. These Sabbath services began with prayer and song, and then a recitation of the Shema: "Hear, O Israel: The Lord our God is one Lord" (Deuteronomy 6:4). After the recitation, the leader of the synagogue would bring out the Torah scroll for a reading, with males assigned as voice before the congregation on a rotating basis. After the Torah reading, a selection from the Prophets would be read, with the assigned reader offering a sermon thereafter. Services would close with the Aaronic blessing if a priest was present to read it: "The Lord bless thee, and keep thee: the Lord make his face shine upon thee, and be gracious unto thee: the Lord lift up his countenance upon thee, and give thee peace" (Numbers 6:24–26). Because priests were associated with temple service in Jerusalem, it would have been common, I think, for congregations in the Galilee, where Jesus grew up, to go without this blessing at the end of their Sabbath service where a rabbi rather than a priest was conducting the service.

Undoubtedly, Jesus, from a very young age, was raised to attend these Sabbath services, which continued among the Jewish people even after a remnant had returned to Jerusalem from Babylon and built the second temple. The New Testament makes it clear that Jesus never forsook that habit. In fact, Matthew wrote that "Jesus went about all Galilee, teaching in their synagogues, and preaching the gospel of the kingdom" (Matthew 4:23). Jesus was recognized by many as a rabbi extraordinarily skilled in His teaching.

Early in His ministry, not long after His forty-day fast, Jesus attended Sabbath synagogue services in Nazareth. Perhaps because this was His hometown synagogue, He would have been assigned the reading from the scroll of the prophet Isaiah, and He went in order to fulfill that Sabbath teaching assignment. When the moment in the service came for His reading, He stood and read these words: "The Spirit of the Lord God is upon me; because the Lord hath anointed me to preach good tidings unto the meek; he hath sent me to bind up the brokenhearted, to proclaim liberty to the captives, and the opening of the prison to them that are bound" (Isaiah 61:1–2). And then, according to custom, He sat down before bearing a very short testimony: "This day is this scripture fulfilled in your ears" (Luke 4:21). The Lord's work of salvation in the meridian of time began with a Sabbath scripture reading and a testimony before a congregation of hometown worshippers.

John recorded how, on another Sabbath, Jesus taught a lesson that expanded upon that testimony of salvation. It was soon after the miracle of the loaves and the fishes. Jesus had quietly taken His leave of the crowd so as to avoid their growing desire for Him to assume a secular leadership role. The crowd sought Him in Capernaum, where they found Him attending Sabbath services. Jesus, knowing the crowd sought Him in order to receive more bread from Him, taught them to "labour not for the meat which perisheth, but for that meat which endureth unto everlasting life, which the Son of man shall give unto you" (John 6:27). The crowd insisted that they wanted bread, pointing out that God had provided manna from heaven for the people in the time of Moses. "And Jesus said unto them, I am the bread of life: he that cometh to me shall never hunger; and he that believeth on me shall never thirst. . . . For I came down from heaven, not to do mine own will, but the will of him that sent me" (John 6:35–8) Jesus challenged them to set aside their temporal concerns and believe He came from God, our Father in Heaven, to provide a way for God's children to receive His greatest gift, which is eternal life.

Anticipating His eventual atoning sacrifice and the ordinance He would establish for all future Sabbath services, Jesus went on to teach a central lesson of the gospel: "Then Jesus said unto them, . . . except ye eat the flesh of the Son of man, and drink his blood, ye have no life in you. Whoso eateth my flesh, and drinketh my blood, hath eternal life; and I will raise him up at the last day. For my flesh is meat indeed, and my blood is drink indeed. He that eateth my flesh, and drinketh my blood, dwelleth in me, and I in him. As the living Father hath sent me, and I live by the Father: so he that eateth me, even he shall live by me. This is that bread which came down from heaven: not as your fathers did eat manna, and are dead: he that eateth of this bread shall live for ever" (John 6:53–58).

In this way, Jesus taught His disciples that the work of salvation in the synagogue service held on the Sabbath was for them personally. As their personal savior sent from their Father in Heaven, He offered them eternal life upon condition of their choosing to believe in Him and repent. All four Gospels include the story about the instigation of the sacrament as an ordinance for those who choose to follow Christ. Likewise, the Nephite prophets explicitly detail the importance of Sabbath services and the sacramental ordinance in the spiritual lives of Christians. Moroni wrote: "And after they had been received unto baptism, and were wrought upon and cleansed by the power of the Holy Ghost, they were numbered among the people of the church of Christ . . . that they might be remembered and nourished by the good word of God, to keep them in the right way, to keep them continually watchful unto prayer, relying alone upon the merits of Christ, who was the author and the finisher of their faith. And the church did meet together oft, to fast and to pray, and to speak one with another concerning the welfare of their souls. And they did meet together oft to partake of bread and wine, in remembrance of the Lord Jesus. . . . And their meetings were conducted by the church after the manner of the workings of the Spirit, and by the power of the Holy Ghost; for as the power of the Holy Ghost led them whether to preach, or to exhort, or to pray, or to supplicate, or to sing, even so it was done" (Moroni 6:4–6, 9).

Modern-day prophets and apostles have likewise taught us to remember the Sabbath day, exhorting us to keep it holy, with particular attention to church services. In a general conference, Elder David Bednar taught:

> That we might more fully keep ourselves unspotted from the world, we are commanded to go to the house of prayer and offer up our sacraments upon the Lord's holy day. . . .
>
> The sacramental emblems are sanctified in remembrance of Christ's purity, of our total dependence upon His Atonement, and of our responsibility to so honor our ordinances and covenants that we can "stand spotless before [Him] at the last day. . . .

The ordinance of the sacrament is a holy, repeated invitation to repent sincerely and be renewed spiritually. The act of partaking the sacrament in and of itself does not remit sins. But as we conscientiously prepare and participate in this holy ordinance with a broken heart and contrite spirit, the promise is that we may *always* have the Spirit of the Lord to be with us. And by the sanctifying power of the Holy Ghost as our constant companion, we can *always* retain a remission of our sins. ("Always Retain a Remission of Your Sins," *Ensign*, May 2016)

If we are sincere about becoming disciples of the Lord, we should do what our Savior did and hallow the Sabbath as a sign between ourselves and our God that we are sincere. Through my opportunities to participate in prayerful planning of Sabbath-day services, I've gained a personal witness that these meetings are conducted according to the workings of the Spirit. When we follow the Messiah and accept assignments on Sunday to preach, pray, supplicate, or sing, we are doing the will of the living God. He has arranged for the priesthood to always be present to bless the emblems of His body and blood, thus ensuring that His blessings will keep us, His face will shine upon us, and His countenance will be lifted up upon us. Go for the full meeting time so that you can be nourished by the good word of God. Be numbered among the people of the Church of Christ on the Sabbath so that during the week you will keep in the right way and be continually watchful unto prayer. Sabbath worship is designed to help you rely alone upon the merits of Christ. It is the work of our personal salvation. It is how you partake of the bread of life and thereby always retain a remission of your sins. On the Sabbath, you will hear the preaching of good tidings—that the brokenhearted are bound up, the captives are offered liberty, and the prisons are opened. By accepting the call to Sabbath worship, we receive the blessings promised by Isaiah to those who come to the Messiah: those who mourn shall have beauty for ashes, the oil of joy to transcend mourning, the garment of praise for the spirit of heaviness, and they will become the trees of righteousness or the planting of the Lord (see Isaiah 61:3).

CAPERNAUM

Capernaum was the center of the Savior's Galilean ministry. In fact, the Gospel writers call Capernaum "his own city," referring to Jesus. It appears Capernaum was the actual hometown of several of Jesus's disciples, including Peter, Andrew, James, John, and Matthew. Capernaum was a crossroads with toll booths for taxation. There would have been royal oversight of the fishing industry here as well, ensuring licensing fees were duly paid. As mentioned, taxation was heavy enough that multiple families would have had to join together to sustain a fishing enterprise on the Sea of Galilee.

Throughout the Gospels, we find Jesus healing and teaching in the synagogue in Capernaum, though the ruins of the first-century synagogue

Ruins of the narrow streets and domiciles of ancient Capernaum

Ruins of the fourth-century-AD synagogue in Capernaum

Jesus would have known are likely underneath the fourth-century synagogue that has been excavated.

The Gospels make mention of many episodes of miraculous healing by
Jesus in Capernaum, all of which are discounted as myth by biblical minimalists. An answer to these biblical minimalists has been advanced by the
late Anglo-American theologian and philosopher Colin Brown. He notes
that in many instances in the Gospels, Jesus was accused by His critics of
working miracles through the power of devils:

> But the Pharisees said, He casteth out devils through the prince
> of the devils. (Matthew 9:34)

> But when the Pharisees heard it, they said, This fellow doth not
> cast out devils, but by Beelzebub the prince of the devils. (Mat-
> thew 12:24)

> And the scribes which came down from Jerusalem said, He hath

Beelzebub, and by the prince of the devils casteth he out devils. (Mark 3:22)

But some of them said, He casteth out devils through Beelzebub the chief of the devils. (Luke 11:15)

Brown's theory resonates with me. He suggests it is unlikely that the Gospel writers, who were promoting Jesus as the Messiah, would make up something so grievous about Him. The Jews of that time would have been very concerned about demons. To be accused of being in league with demonic forces would have been very damaging to one's reputation and character. If the writers of the Gospels were simply producing a manufactured narrative, they would have avoided anything that cast Jesus in a bad light. Therefore, since these writers were far more likely to have reported what the critics of Jesus actually said about Him, it only makes sense that the miracles actually took place. The mere fact that Jesus's critics accused Him of working miracles, albeit through the devil, indicates that obviously something supernatural and powerful took place, something the Pharisees of the day were loath to attribute to God but had no natural explanation for. The fact that they don't deny the miracles but try to cast aspersions on the source is evidence that the miracles took place. Biblical minimalists who simply assert that Jesus was a good teacher and performed no miracles are not making an assertion with historical validity, for that is not what the people of His own era thought about Him.

These miraculous healing episodes in Capernaum include a man possessed of an unclean spirit at synagogue (see Luke 4:31–6; Mark 1:21–8), Peter's mother-in-law healed of a fever (see Luke 4:38–9), and the healing of the Roman centurion's servant (see Luke 7:1–10; Matthew 8:5). But one particular healing episode in Capernaum deserves special mention: "And again he entered into Capernaum after some days; and it was noised that he was in the house. And straightway many were gathered together, insomuch that there was no room to receive them, no, not so much as about the door: and he preached the word unto them. And they come unto him, bringing one sick of the palsy, which was borne of four. And when they could not come nigh unto him for the press, they uncovered the roof where he was: and when they had broken it up, they let down the bed wherein the sick of the palsy lay. When Jesus saw their faith, he said unto the sick of the palsy, Son, thy sins be forgiven thee" (Mark 2:1–5).

What was it Jesus saw that confirmed the faith of these men? Faith is not blind, wishful thinking. It is not unquestioning belief. Faith is not imposed upon us by birth, parentage, or culture. God does not compel us to have faith. All people are equally able to have faith because all people are equally able to choose what they believe or desire to believe. Those who desire something better in this life can give place for the word of God in their hearts. The four friends of the man with palsy chose to believe what they had heard about Jesus, that He was a healer. The sick man chose to believe in what Jesus offered him, which was forgiveness of sin. All acted upon their beliefs by overcoming the obstacles that stood between them

The Apostle Peter's neighborhood in Capernaum

and the Savior. By doing so, they entered into an experiment upon Christ's word. They reached out to have a relationship of love with God. This was the faith Christ saw in them.

This episode took place at a home in Capernaum, probably Peter's home, where Jesus would likely have stayed when He was in town. The possible location of Peter's home has been discovered in the ruins of Capernaum, so we can see this place and get an idea of what it must have been like when crowds surrounded the house, filled the street outside, and blocked the way to Jesus, forcing these men to carry their friend up on the roof.

The nearby streets are narrow. A few dozen people would have effectively blocked entry to the house. Standing in the ruins of Capernaum today, one can easily imagine how hard a task it would have been to get a palsied patient to the rooftop of Peter's abode. These men were not acting on a whim or hoping that perhaps Jesus would or could be of some help. Rather, they were well aware of who He was and what He could do.

The Apostle Peter's home in Capernaum, covered by a modern Catholic church

Statue of the Apostle Peter at the modern-day archeological park of Capernaum

They already had a relationship of love with the Savior and were acting on faith. No matter how hard the task, they were going to bring their friend to Jesus so He could minister to the palsied man. This is what Jesus saw in them, and this is what He responded to as He healed their friend. It is the same relationship He asks us to have with Him today: Will we love Him enough to overcome all barriers? For those who sincerely seek Him, He will be found no matter how much biblical minimalists would have it otherwise.

Ruins of Capernaum showing how narrow the streets would have been

The Mount of Beatitudes

On a Galilean hill like the one pictured below, Jesus delivered the Sermon on the Mount. The state of blessedness described by Jesus at the beginning of this sermon is essentially a condition of humility. People who are poor in spirit, meek, mourning, hungering for righteousness, merciful, pure in heart, peacemakers, and persecuted all have something in common: they have come to a point in their lives where they desire something they know themselves powerless to create. They are prepared to rely on God. I have learned that if I want to achieve the state of blessedness proposed in the Beatitudes, I must embrace the work required to humble myself enough to learn to embody at least one of these characteristics.

Meekness, for instance, is to me a combination of gentleness and humility that fits the admonition the Savior gave to the Prophet Joseph Smith: "Learn of me, and listen to my words; walk in the meekness of my spirit,

A possible site for the Sermon on the Mount near the Sea of Galilee

and you shall have peace in me" (D&C 19:23) It takes meekness to embrace the grace of God, which my Bible dictionary defines as the "divine means of help or strength, given through the bounteous mercy and love of Jesus Christ" (Bible Dictionary, "Grace"). Grace is the gift from Jesus to each of us that allows us to be resurrected and, if we are repentant, live in a condition of everlasting life. In mortality, grace gives us the strength and assistance we need to do good works that would otherwise be left undone if we were left to our own means. This is why the Savior said the meek will inherit the earth. The Greek word translated as "meek" in the Sermon on the Mount means to be gentle, forgiving, or benevolent. Those who possess these qualities are the people who have real influence among their fellow men. Joseph Smith revealed that real power and influence is maintained only by "long-suffering, gentleness, meekness, and love unfeigned" (D&C 121:41).

If achieving this state of blessedness seems unreachable to you, try concentrating on one of the eight characteristics of the blesseds identified in the Beatitudes. My personal focus is on mercy. I try daily to remember how Jesus taught that those who are merciful will have mercy given to them. I know that in each encounter I have with others, my faults and theirs will be evident. When their faults seem to get in my way or keep me from doing what I plan or wish to do, I need to remind myself to offer them mercy and that my faults might be equally vexing to them. I have more difficulty being peaceful, or pure in heart, but merciful seems to be a trait I can reach toward. I have great hope that as I strive to increase that one trait, I will be shown by the Spirit ways to improve and develop the other traits, for all are intertwined.

The Sermon on the Mount is the ultimate expression of the deepest human desire: that the endless cycle of human cruelty come to an end. This repeated pattern and its dire consequences can be seen throughout the scriptures. The Flood was the necessary intervention of God at the time of Noah because violence was sweeping humanity and the rising generation stood no chance of being able to make a real choice about God. The Nephite civilization died because it became addicted to violence. Did

Jesus make a difference in this endless cycle with what He taught? Did Jesus have a lasting impact on the course of history merely by teaching that real influence is wielded by the meek and merciful?

To answer that, we need to understand that the cultural world Jesus lived in was shaped, principally, by the deeds of Alexander the Great and the Hellenizing influences promoted by Greek and Roman civilization for centuries thereafter. Alexander was called "the Great" because he did more of what was then considered the ultimate act of achievement than anyone before or probably since: he conquered. So who had the greater, or more lasting, effect on the history of the world—Alexander the Great, the military genius and conqueror of the known world, or Jesus, the rabbi who taught with authority and gave His life for others?

At first glance, it might appear that Alexander the Great, with his "might makes right" philosophy, had a greater impact on the history of mankind. The Old Testament makes it clear that the second temple period, with the rebuilt temple and reconstituted Jewish culture in Jerusalem, was

View toward the Sea of Galilee past the porch of the church built by the Italian dictator Mussolini to commemorate the Sermon on the Mount

The Galilean sky seen from the gardens on the Mount of Beatitudes

The ceiling of the church on the Mount of Beatitudes

a necessary antecedent to the birth, life, and death of the Savior. He had to be born, raised, and die in and around the Holy City. But after the second temple was built during Alexander's lifetime a few hundred years before Christ's birth, the Greeks conquered Jerusalem and put the image of Zeus in the temple, which the Jews of that era accommodated. More lastingly, the Jews worked with the Greeks to corrupt the temple treasury, allowing its sacred funds to be siphoned off for the enrichment of the wealthy classes, both Jew and Gentile, a practice which continued on into Jesus's lifetime. At least twice in the scriptures, we see Jesus publicly protest the corruption of the temple treasury through this institutionalized embezzlement. These bold actions are most likely the primary reason He was targeted by the priestly class for execution.

The Maccabees, founders of the Hasmonean dynasty into which King Herod eventually married, struck the first blow in history for religious freedom with their revolt in the second century BC against the Seleucid Empire, which occupied Israel at the time and had corrupted Judean religious practice with Greek influences. Upon achieving victory, the Maccabees were empowered to clean up the accounting for the temple treasury and refurbish the second temple. (Hanukah celebrates their rededication of the temple and the miracle that occurred when a one-day supply of consecrated oil for lighting the Menorah lasted eight days.)

Sadly, their attempt to reestablish traditional religious and temple practices was short-lived. The Hasmoneans eventually accommodated Hellenization and all of its practices, including owning and operating the temple treasury for their own aggrandizement. Herod the Great was the last of the line of Hasmonean rulers, though he was merely an in-law. He managed to get the Romans to declare him to be "king of the Jews," but to exercise that title, he too had to conquer, Greek-style, the people he ruled. His cruelty in crushing rebellion has a well-earned infamy. He tracked rebels down to the last man, even to the point of sending his troops over the edges of cliffs to kill escapees hiding in cliff-face caves. Herod never lost his paranoia about whether an alternative king of the Jews would be found or designated, and, eventually, this drove him literally crazy and led him to compulsively kill those closest to him. In fact, he killed his first and most beloved wife, the Hasmonean princess, only to mourn her for the rest of his life.

The Jews were not naturally believers in Hellenistic social order, which would have meant resigning themselves to the absolute rule of the powerful. The Greek worldview placed human wisdom at the center of the universe, while the Jews understood that all blessings flowed from God. The Greeks believed they could triumph over the world through sheer willpower. The Jews understood that without God, life was meaningless. The Greeks believed they prospered by "management of the creature" (Alma 30:17), and this was their supreme goal. Like biblical minimalists, they denied the possibility of a life beyond. The Jews were raised to believe in the Abrahamic covenant and that every person had value because he or she was created in the image of and loved by God. Therefore, every human had a self-organized destiny, wrought together with God by one's own actions and determination. Thus, in every person resided a hope of the promise for the realization of justice in this life and the next.

When Jesus undertook a ministry among His brothers and sisters, He taught principles fashioned for this Jewish audience using the ethical backdrop of the Abrahamic covenant. He carefully selected His teaching methods. His call to people was simple: the time has come to be open to something new. His teaching was always gentle and never threatening. He offered His audience a new start, a cleansing, and He taught them that the gift of the Spirit would help them realize their potential. His teaching was universally recognized as authoritative because virtually everyone He taught had witnessed one of the miracles He'd wrought. He spoke only to the powerless; in front of the elite, He often chose to be silent, such as when He refused to answer Herod Antipas during the sham trial before He was crucified. When He spoke, His words were simple and came directly from the Old Testament: do justice, love mercy, walk humbly, and you will be happy. He stated or implied that power and conquest are illusions and that the

Hellenistic (and Roman) emphasis on "might makes right" was pointless and delusional.

So, which worldview has come to dominate modern ethics? Are we Hellenists who pursue fulfillment through successive conquests? Or do we follow the Christian ethic and seek integrity, justice, equity, and the rule of law, even if that pursuit comes by way of personal sacrifice? People today suffer from natural cataclysms and human-caused disasters just as they did two thousand years ago. While there is never a satisfactory temporal explanation for why people must suffer, Christianity teaches us that we never need suffer alone because we can always depend on divine help. The Greco-Roman urge toward intense competition for a victory in a zero-sum world, though it is alive and well in the modern world, seems increasingly illusory because it never satisfies or lasts. We are fortunate when we come to understand that another person's success doesn't detract from our own possibilities. On the societal level, the Christian rejection of power because of the inherent evil of pursuing self-interest and of the wickedness of war has created a modern pressure to make peace and render justice. We are, to be sure, imperfect at living this ethic, but it has become the standard by which nations are judged. I think even biblical minimalists would agree that what Jesus taught has outlasted how Alexander the Great lived.

TABGHA

The last site of Jesus's Galilean ministry, Tabgha, is said to be where the resurrected Savior begins teaching His Apostles during the forty days or so between the Resurrection and the Day of Pentecost.

After the heartbreak of the Crucifixion, during which Peter allows his fears to chill his heart into a betrayal of the Savior, and despite the exhilaration of the Resurrection, when left to his agency, Peter goes back to fishing and takes six Apostles with him. They spend a fruitless night fishing only to have a man shout from shore at sunrise that they should cast from the other side of the boat. Immediately, they catch more than they can easily handle, and John, the author of the account, claims the initial insight that their shore-based benefactor must be Jesus. Peter swims the one hundred yards to shore, the sooner to greet the Savior. There, his conscience is thrice stung when Jesus asks three times, "Simon, lovest thou me?" Peter insists three times "Thou knowest that I love thee." Jesus does not contradict but says only, "Feed my sheep" (John 21).

Charity is not an intellectual exercise or emotion. We cannot feel charity, nor is it merely a pleasant thought experiment. You cannot store charity or borrow it from someone. You cannot fall into love or have a charitable relationship without effort because you must constantly apply yourself to create love. Peter felt he loved Christ, and intellectually he knew that Jesus was resurrected, but he could not truly love the Savior unless he worked at it like he had formerly worked at fishing. Charity is something we *do*. It is a principle we live by. It is the active expression of our faith, our love for God.

Jesus demonstrated charity throughout His ministry. On the eve of His arrest, Jesus taught the powerful lesson that charity requires action when He washed His disciples' feet. And He made it clear that if we are to be His, we must emulate His actions: "If I then, your Lord and Master, have washed your feet; ye also ought to wash one another's feet. For I have given you an example, that ye should do as I have done to you. Verily, verily, I say unto you, The servant is not greater than his lord; neither he that is sent greater than he that sent him. If ye know these things, happy are ye if ye do them" (John 13:14–17).

If we fail to have charity, we fail to be like Jesus or to know who He is. Charity is the highest of standards and is found at the end of the Sermon on the Mount, the greatest lecture on charity ever given. "Not every one that saith unto me, Lord, Lord, shall enter into the Kingdom of Heaven; but he that doeth the will of my Father which is in heaven. Many will say to me in that day, Lord, Lord, have we not prophesied in thy name? And in thy name have cast out devils? And in thy name done many wonderful works? And then will I profess unto them, I never knew you: depart from me, ye that work iniquity" (Matthew 7:21–23). Nothing can take the place of charity. Charity is how the world can recognize a Christian. Charity is how to be a Christian. Charity is the only means available to teach Christianity.

Like Peter, we each must make a choice between Christ and our worldly pursuits. Success in worldly pursuits, even on the scale described in this story, with nets sagging with fish, must be considered in light of Christ's question to Peter: "Simon, lovest thou me more than these" fish? And like Peter, we cannot get by with mere words of reassurance: "Yea Lord, thou knowest I love thee." For He has said, "He that hath my commandments, and keepeth them, he it is that loveth me" (see John 14:21). And this is His commandment: that we love one another as He loved us (see John 13:34). This is not to say that if fishing is our livelihood we must give it up in the pursuit of charity but rather that we must find a way to both fish

The shore of the Sea of Galilee where the resurrected Jesus met some of His Apostles after they spent a fruitless night fishing

and live life with charity, making every interaction with every person we meet one of loving service informed by patience, kindness, forgiveness, and meekness.

THE MOUNT OF OLIVES

The modern traveler driving from the Galilee to Jerusalem will probably follow the Jordan River down to the Dead Sea and then make a right turn on Highway 1. This modern freeway climbs from 1400 feet below sea level at the Dead Sea to 2500 feet above sea level at Jerusalem. The highway then tunnels through the Mount of Olives, emerging to a remarkable view of Jerusalem focused on the Dome of the Rock atop Temple Mount, or Mount Moriah. When the traveler arrives, the weather is usually good, as noted by the Psalmist: "Great is the Lord, and greatly to be praised in the city of

View of Jerusalem from the Mount of Olives, including the Jewish cemetery at its base

The Judean Desert

our God, in the mountain of his holiness. Beautiful for situation, the joy of the whole earth, is mount Zion" (Psalms 48:1–2).

Jerusalem is favored by fifteen inches of rain each year, with the occasional snowfall, but there's plenty of sunshine. Neither generally too hot nor too cold, the climate here is a stark contrast to the other side of the Mount of Olives, where the Judean Desert begins.

Presumably, the biblical minimalist would not disagree with the Psalmist about the beauty of Jerusalem, though perhaps not taking the favorable impression of the Holy City as far as this: "By the rivers of Babylon, there we sat down, yea, we wept, when we remembered Zion. . . . For there they that carried us away captive required of us a song, . . . saying, sing us one of the songs of Zion. How shall we sing the Lord's song in a strange land? If I forget thee, O Jerusalem, let my right hand forget her cunning. If I do not remember thee, let my tongue cleave to the roof of my mouth; if I prefer not Jerusalem above my chief joy" (Psalms 137:1–6).

According to Jewish tradition, a dove brought Noah the twig of an olive tree from the Mount of Olives, signaling an end to the Flood. The Mount of Olives is first mentioned in the Old Testament as the beginning of King David's flight from his son Absalom, who had instigated a rebellion against his father: "And David went up by the ascent of the Mount of Olives and wept as he went up" (2 Samuel 15:30).

View of the Mount of Olives as seen looking east from Old Jerusalem past the Dome of the Rock on Temple Mount

At the end of His life, Jesus would take King David's route in reverse as He entered Jerusalem on Palm Sunday. It was the Mount of Olives Ezekiel saw in a vision as the place where the "glory of the Lord went up from the midst of the city" (Ezekiel 11:23) after the desecration of the temple by the invading Babylonian army. It was on this sacred

The Dome of the Rock as seen from the Mount of Olives

mountain that King Solomon built altars to the gods of his foreign wives, instigating a practice of idol worship that remained until the reign of King Josiah. It was from the Mount of Olives that Jesus viewed Jerusalem and wept over it.

During Passion Week, Jesus traveled repeatedly from Bethany, home of Lazarus, Martha, and Mary to Jerusalem, over the Mount of Olives, including on Palm Sunday. The Garden of Gethsemane is at the foot of the Mount of Olives, and Jesus ascended to heaven from the center of the Mount of Olives (see Acts 1:9–12). Today, the most obvious aspect of the Mount of Olives is the numerous graves at its base. There are over 150,000 graves, including tombs believed to be for Absalom (David's rebellious son) and the prophets Zechariah, Haggai, and Malachi on the upper slope.

Jewish burials on the Mount of Olives began during the first temple period (1200–586 BC) and continue even today. During the pre-Zionist era (considered before 1897), older Jews from around the world moved to Jerusalem in order to live out their lives and be buried on the Mount of Olives. Those who could not be buried on the Mount of Olives often had their graves sprinkled with dirt harvested from the mount and sent to their families for that purpose. Burials on the Mount of Olives are based upon the Jewish tradition that when the Messiah comes, He will stand on the Mount of Olives and the Resurrection of the dead will begin there.

TEMPLE MOUNT

Across the Kidron Valley from the Mount of Olives stands Temple Mount, known anciently as Mount Moriah. Nothing about what makes Temple Mount important to monotheists is accepted by biblical minimalists. To care about Temple Mount, an individual must be a believer in monotheism; all three monotheistic religions have important traditions related to this place.

Jewish tradition holds that this is where the Garden of Eden was located and therefore where Adam made sacrifice to God. It also holds that Noah sacrificed here after the floodwaters receded. The first actual mention of Mount Moriah in the Old Testament is in conjunction with the story of Abraham's would-be sacrifice of his son Isaac, as found in the twenty-second chapter of Genesis: "And it came to pass after these things, that God did tempt Abraham, and said unto him, Abraham: and he said, behold, here I am. And he said, Take now thy son, thine only son Isaac, whom thou lovest, and get thee into the land of Moriah; and offer him there for a burnt offering upon one of the mountains which I will tell thee of. And Abraham rose up early in the morning, and saddled his ass, and took two of his young men with him, and Isaac his son, and clave the wood for the burnt offering, and rose up, and went unto the place of which God had told him" (verses 1–3).

For members of The Church of Jesus Christ of Latter-day Saints, this story takes on added significance. From the book of Abraham (part of the Latter-day canon of scripture), they know that Abraham himself was to be sacrificed on an altar. It was this near-death experience at the hands of the pagan priests of Ur, where Abraham lived, that drove him into the arms of the true and living God. To then have this same God, who Abraham had learned to follow and worship, ask him for the life of his only son, the son he loved so dearly, is beyond irony. It is a hard story to read and understand: "And Abraham took the wood of the burnt offering, and laid it upon Isaac his son; and he took the fire in his hand, and a knife; and they went both of them together. And Isaac spake unto Abraham his father, and said, My father: and he said, Here am I, my son. And he said, Behold the fire and the wood: but where is the lamb for a burnt offering? And Abraham said, My son, God will provide himself a lamb for a burnt offering: so they went both of them together. And they came to the place which God had told him of; and Abraham built an altar there, and laid the wood in order, and bound Isaac his son, and laid him on the altar upon the wood. And Abraham stretched forth his hand, and took the knife to slay his son. And the angel of the Lord called unto him out of heaven, and said, Abraham, Abraham: and he said, Here am I. And he said, Lay not thine hand upon the lad, neither do thou any thing unto him: for now I know that thou fearest God, seeing thou hast not withheld thy son, thine only son from me. And Abraham lifted up his eyes, and looked, and behold behind him a ram caught in a thicket by his horns: and Abraham went and took the ram, and offered him up for a burnt offering in the stead of his son" (Genesis 22:6–13).

In this poignant story between father and son, it is made clear that Isaac, who was old enough to carry the wood and ask the question about what was to be sacrificed, was also old enough to escape from his very elderly father. Abraham would not have been able to bind and put Isaac on the altar without his son's compliance. Abraham had bargained with God in the past for the life of Lot, his nephew, asking for Sodom to be spared destruction if but a few righteous were found there. Abraham is described as a friend of God, and yet, in this story, there is no mention of discussion or bargaining. Both Abraham and Isaac implicitly accept God's direction, apparently fully intending to comply with the command to offer up as a sacrifice the life of a son/self. No wonder this story is often called the most fearsome account in scripture. To enter into a relationship with God and to strive to be God's friend is to begin to understand what one must be willing to give up in order to love God or have faith in Him. No wonder biblical minimalists want nothing to do with this sort of obedience and fellowship. But it is in this kind of relationship that the rewards of obedience to God become clear: "And the angel of the Lord called unto Abraham out of heaven the second time, and said, By myself have I sworn, saith the Lord, for because thou hast done this thing, and hast not withheld thy son, thine only son: that in blessing I will bless thee, and in multiplying I will multiply thy seed as the stars of the heaven, and as the sand which is upon the sea shore; and thy seed shall possess the gate of his enemies; and in thy seed shall all the nations of the earth be blessed; because thou hast obeyed my voice" (Genesis 22:15–18).

Mount Moriah is sacred to the principal three monotheistic religions because it was here that Abraham and Isaac secured the blessings of under-standing the power of obedience to God to change the meaning of human life. Here, mankind changed its understanding of the purpose of life and the potential of each individual human history. This understanding has blessed all of the nations of the earth despite the very modern and only recently articulated disbelief of biblical minimalists. One must be clear, however, that the monotheistic religions do not agree on all things, cer-tainly not about what happened on Mount Moriah. For instance, Muslims insist the son Abraham loved, the son to be offered as sacrifice, was Ish-mael, not Isaac. Further, Muslims do not necessarily accept that the would-be sacrifice occurred on Mount Moriah; they prefer a mountain closer to Mecca. And Muslims do not accept that there ever was a temple on Mount Moriah. Nor do they agree with Ezekiel that a third temple will be built here.

The great monotheistic traditions—Judaism, Islam, and Christianity—have all had their turn at governing Mount Moriah, and none have had an unblemished record of justice and equity while in charge. According to the Old Testament, King David first arranged to buy the property on top of the mount and bring it under Jewish rule. His successor several generations later, King Hezekiah, saw Mount Moriah surrounded by 185,000 Assyrian troops and heard the prophet Isaiah state that those troops, despite their overwhelming appearance, would never shoot an arrow on the mount. About a century later, however, the prophet Jeremiah saw the mount sur-rounded by Babylonian troops and prophesied that the battle would go against the Jews and King Zedekiah. Jewish hegemony over Mount Moriah occurred principally before Christ and therefore before there were Muslims and Christians, with the exception of the half century since the Six-Day War in 1967. Twice, Jewish rule over Temple Mount was ended by Gentile armies waging brutal siege warfare against Jerusalem (the Babylonians in 586 BC and the Romans in 70 AD). Both times, Jewish prophets proclaimed that God permitted the destruction of the Jewish temple because the people had become too wicked to sustain meaningful worship.

This is how the Prophet Jeremiah describes the people of Jerusalem just before the Babylonian conquest:"But this people hath a revolting and a rebellious heart; they are revolted and gone. Neither say they in their heart, Let us now fear the Lord our God, that giveth rain, both the former and the latter, in his season: he reserveth unto us the appointed weeks of the harvest. Your iniquities have turned away these things, and your sins have withholden good things from you. For among my people are found wicked men: they lay wait, as he that setteth snares; they set a trap, they catch men. As a cage is full of birds, so are their houses full of deceit: therefore they are become great, and waxen rich. They are waxen fat, they shine: yea, they overpass the deeds of the wicked: they judge not the cause, the cause of the fatherless, yet they prosper; and the right of the needy do they not judge. Shall I not visit for these things? saith the Lord: shall not my soul be avenged on such a nation as this? A wonderful and horrible thing is committed in the land; the prophets prophesy falsely, and the priests bear rule by their means; and my people love to have it so: and what will ye do in the end thereof?" (Jeremiah 5:23–31).

Because the people of the kingdom of Judah had become fat by failing to look to the needs of the fatherless and poor, and because they loved having prophets and priests who flattered them with deceit, Jeremiah prophesied a bitter end for the city: "And I will make void the counsel of Judah and Jerusalem in this place; and I will cause them to fall by the sword before their enemies, and by the hands of them that seek their lives: and their carcases will I give to be meat for the fowls of the heaven, and for the beasts of the earth. And I will make this city desolate, and an hissing; every one that passeth thereby shall be astonished and hiss because of all the plagues thereof. And I will cause them to eat the flesh of their sons and the flesh of their daughters, and they shall eat every one the flesh of his friend in the siege and straitness, wherewith their enemies, and they that seek their lives, shall straiten them" (Jeremiah 19:7–9).

It pretty much happened that way. War is never pretty, but the wars over Jerusalem have tended to be among the most bloody and cruel. Mount

Moriah was put under siege seventy times over the millennia. In 70 AD, the Romans burned the second temple after it was refurbished by King Herod the Great and destroyed the city, ending the Jewish reign on Mount Moriah for the next nearly two thousand years.

During the Roman siege of Jerusalem, Titus, the Roman general, crucified every Jew caught escaping the starvation conditions in the city. As many as five hundred wooden crucifixes were erected on the Mount of Olives each day, leading to the deforestation of Jerusalem's hillsides. Temple Mount was under pagan/Roman rule for a few hundred years, with a temple to Jupiter on the top of the mount, until the Byzantine era when Constantine converted the Roman empire to Christianity in 337 AD. The Byzantine Christians destroyed the pagan temple and left Temple Mount barren as a witness to Jesus's statement about Jerusalem before His own Crucifixion: "And Jesus went out and departed from the temple: and his disciples came to him for to shew him the buildings of the temple. And Jesus said unto them, See ye not all these things? verily I say unto you, there shall not be left here one stone upon another, that shall not be thrown down" (Matthew 24:1–2).

In general, Christians, including the Byzantines, agreed with the Hebrew scriptures about the happenings on Temple Mount, including that it was Isaac who was offered there. And Christians accept that both the first and second temples were built on Mount Moriah and that a third temple will be erected at some future date.

Ultimately, Byzantine rule gave way to Islamic invasion, which remained the regulating power over Temple Mount for more than one thousand years, except for brief periods of Crusader rule, until the end of World War I and the demise of the Ottoman Empire. The century since then has seen Christian, Muslim, and then Jewish rule on Temple Mount, with the British Mandate, then Jordanian rule, and finally Israeli rule since the Six-Day War in 1967.

Because Muslims have been the principal rulers of Temple Mount (which is known as Haram al-Sharif, or "Noble Sanctuary" to Muslims) for most of the last 1400 years, the oldest structure on Temple Mount (perhaps in all of Jerusalem) now is the Dome of the Rock, which is the third holiest shrine for Muslims, who believe that the ongoing presence on Temple Mount of the Dome of the Rock (Qubbat al-Sakhrah) is evidence of divine approval for their mode of worship.

The Dome of the Rock is not a mosque but rather a shrine to the Abrahamic creation story (which is shared with Judaic tradition), the Abraham and Isaac/Ishmael sacrifice story, and the ascension to heaven of the prophet Muhammad, founder of Islam. The location of this shrine is said to have been designated by Ka'ab al-Ahbār, a Jewish rabbi who converted to Islam and advised Caliph Umar ibn Al-Khattāb about the meaning of the "farthest mosque," which is identified in the Quran as the site of Muhammed's heavenly ascension. Ka'ab al-Ahbār believed that the "farthest mosque" must be identical with the site of the former Jewish temples in Jerusalem. It is puzzling how Muslims can maintain that there never were Jewish temples on Temple Mount and that the "farthest mosque" must be where those temples were built—on Temple Mount.

Jews and Christians, however, believe that the prophet Ezekiel in the Old Testament prophesied that a third temple would be built on Mount Moriah. Some believe that only God can build the third temple, while others assert that this temple must be built by people in order to usher in the appearance of the Messiah (Jewish) or the Second Coming of Christ (Christian). It is this intense competition of beliefs about Temple Mount that prevents any peaceful solution to the ongoing conflicts in the Holy Land. It seems there can never be a proposal for Temple Mount that pleases all monotheists.

Most recently, Jewish rule over Temple Mount was reestablished during the Six-Day War, in 1967. This was the most recent siege of Temple Mount by armed forces. Once the Israeli army had control of all of East Jerusalem, the leading rabbis in Jerusalem proclaimed that no Jew was to set foot on Mount Moriah. They reasoned that since no one really knew where the Holy of Holies of the first and second temples might have been located, one could unknowingly tread on sacred ground. Therefore, all foot traffic (at least by Jews) was to be avoided. This declaration, no matter how biblical minimalists might deride it, has had the welcome effect of calming Islamic community fears about the immediate future of Temple Mount.

Israeli authorities have granted Muslim control of the sacred buildings on Temple Mount to the leading Islamic clerics in Jerusalem since 1967 with the proviso that the site always be made available for peaceful visits by tourists. Generally, Muslim authorities have complied with those terms, though they often keep people from visiting Temple Mount during the five times daily when Muslims gather for prayer.

The Dome of the Rock stands on the platform built atop Temple Mount two thousand years ago by King Herod the Great. The most visible section of the retaining walls that support this platform and the holiest site accessible to Jews is the Western Wall, formerly referred to as the Wailing Wall. The destruction of the Jewish temple was traumatic for the surviving Jewish

population. They came to Jerusalem whenever allowed, stood at the Western Wall, and mourned the loss of the temple, often in tears, which accounts for the name "Wailing Wall" being attributed to this part of the infrastructure supporting what was once the second temple.

The original, massive foundation stones laid during King Herod's temple construction more than two thousand years ago can be seen in the subterranean space opened up by archeologists in the years of Israeli governance of East Jerusalem since the conclusion of the Six-Day War.

The Western (or Wailing) Wall

A close-up of the Western Wall of Temple Mount

For almost two decades prior to the Six-Day War, during Jordanian rule of East Jerusalem, Jews were not allowed to visit this sacred site. Now, Jews come here to pray, often leaving their written devotions in crevices of the Wailing Wall. Once inserted into the Wailing Wall, these prayers become as sacred as scripture and, in Jewish tradition, must be preserved. Therefore, twice each year, these written prayers are gathered into bags and taken to the Jewish cemetery on the Mount of Olives and buried.

While Christians and Jews share

The street paving stones laid at the time of King Herod's reconstruction of Temple Mount dating to the time of Christ

Written prayers tucked into crevices of the Western Wall

a reverence for the Western Wall because of its proximity to the area above Temple Mount where both the first and second temples are thought to have been located, Muslims refer to the Western Wall as the Buraq Wall, referring to the winged steed, Buraq, which Muhammad rode from Mecca to Jerusalem and on up to the heavens and back during his journey to the seventh heaven. The Wailing Wall is below where the steed is thought by some Muslims to have been tethered at some point during the journey.

Obviously, there is disagreement

Detail of structures next to the Dome of the Rock on Temple Mount

among the various adherents of these monotheistic religious traditions. Temple Mount is fraught with the contentions of these competing religions. Several years ago, as I stood with a group of LDS tourists on Temple Mount, listening to our guide teach us about the significance of the site, a young Muslim lad stopped to pick up and throw small stones at us. That religious feeling can overcome judgment and lead to violence, on Temple Mount as well as elsewhere, is tragic. But that observation does not dissuade me from feeling something uniquely compelling whenever I visit Temple Mount.

One bright Sunday morning, I was watching the devotional prayers of Jewish men at the Western Wall and heard the muezzin (Muslim prayer caller) sing out his soulful *adhan* over a loudspeaker located on a minaret near Temple Mount. An adhan is an alert to the Muslim community that prayers are about to begin in the mosque.

Just as that haunting call to prayer ended, the bells of Christian churches in Jerusalem rang out the call to Mass. And I was close enough to the Western Wall to hear the chanting prayers of Jews.

The Al-Aqsa Mosque on Temple Mount

Jewish men praying at the Western Wall

As I listened to these various sounds, I felt a sense of the sacred purpose of all three monotheistic traditions. Unlike biblical minimalists, I don't underestimate the importance of holding a reverence for what is sacred. After the destruction of the first temple, the prophet Ezekiel chastised the Jewish nation for putting "no difference between the holy and profane" (Ezekiel 22:26). He declared that their exile was a result of breaking their covenants with God.

When we treat sacred things lightly, when we maintain no boundary between what is holy and what is profane, we lose the something that makes us more human, more humane. Modern secular society, with its emphasis on a transactional life, where values are at best questioned and are often ignored in the pursuit of material gain, has lost its sense of what really matters. That Sunday morning as I ruminated about the sense of the sacredness inherent in the Jewish prayers, the Muslim call to prayer, and the Christian bells tolling for Mass, I saw a raptor suddenly leave its perch on top of the Western Wall and dive at a group of pigeons roosting along the face. The bird of prey made its kill and flew off with its meal. Nature is, indeed, "red in tooth and claw" (Alfred Lord Tennyson, "In Memoriam AHH," 1850), but men and women are the sons and daughters of God and can choose to believe and act otherwise. It is on Temple Mount where the sacred nature of mankind and the values of the divine are, for me, readily embraceable.

On Temple Mount I can imagine myself listening to Jesus teach His radical doctrine of love: "Ye have heard that it hath been said, Thou shalt love thy neighbour, and hate thine enemy. But I say unto you, Love your enemies, bless them that curse you, do good to them that hate you, and pray for them which despitefully use you, and persecute you; that ye may be the children of your Father which is in heaven: for he maketh his sun to rise on the evil and on the good, and sendeth rain on the just and on the unjust. For if ye love them which love you, what reward have ye? Do not even the publicans the same?" (Matthew 5:43–46). This kind of love has its start in extreme forgiveness, such as that offered by Jesus to His

A canopy over a side entrance to the Dome of the Rock on Temple Mount

tormentors and executioners. No other power on earth can bring peace to Temple Mount.

In finding a sense of the sacred on Temple Mount, I am merely embracing the example of Jesus, who had a special reverence for these precincts. Just after the occurrence of the first recorded miracle He performed (changing water into wine at the wedding in Cana), Jesus attended the Passover Feast in Jerusalem: "And the Jews' passover was at hand, and Jesus went up to Jerusalem, and found in the temple those that sold oxen and sheep and doves, and the changers of money sitting: and when he had made a scourge of small cords, he drove them all out of the temple, and the sheep, and the oxen; and poured out the changers' money, and overthrew the tables; and said unto them that sold doves, Take these things hence; make not my Father's house an house of merchandise. And his disciples remembered that it was written, The zeal of thine house hath eaten me up" (John 2:13–17).

Three years later, at the end of His mortal ministry, Jesus again was in Jerusalem for the Passover Feast and again found a commercial invasion of the sacred precincts of the temple: "And Jesus went into the temple of God, and cast out all them that sold and bought in the temple, and overthrew the tables of the moneychangers, and the seats of them that sold doves, and said unto them, It is written, my house shall be called the house of prayer; but ye have made it a den of thieves" (Matthew 21:12–3).

It is clear from the scriptural record that the second temple cleansing led to considerations by the leaders of Jewish society about how to deal definitively with Jesus: "But when they sought to lay hands on him, they feared the multitude, because they took him for a prophet" (Matthew 21:46).

It is also clear Jesus understood that something was inherently wrong with the way the temple affairs were being administered. His choice of attacking the sale of sacrificial animals and exchange of currency located in the Court of the Gentiles targeted retail that could have been conducted elsewhere, freeing this public space within the temple precincts for worship and prayer.

Beginning when the ark of the covenant had been located in Shiloh, there had been a tendency among those given responsibility for conducting the sacred rituals of sacrifice at the temple to exploit their positions of trust, as seen in the story of Eli's sons. Eli, the high priest who taught Samuel how to hear the voice of God, himself had a man of God (the text does not specify who this is, although the phrase "man of God" generally indicates someone authorized to speak for God) chastise him: "Wherefore kick ye at my sacrifice and at mine offering, which I have commanded in my habitation; and honourest thy sons above me, to make yourselves fat with the chiefest of all the offerings of Israel my people?" (1 Samuel 2:29).

The house of Israel had been commanded to present themselves three times a year at the temple to participate in rituals and services meant to remind the people of their reliance upon God for salvation and to renew their personal relationship with Him. All, both rich and poor, were required to pay for the upkeep of the temple and to bring animals and grains for sacrifice, which were to be purchased only in shekels, the allowed temple currency.

At the time of Jesus, the administration of temple affairs, with its revenues flowing from Jews both in Judea and throughout the Diaspora, had long since been recognized as a ready source of income both for the secular authorities and those who managed to secure appointments among the temple priesthood. With administrative authority at the temple came the ability to franchise out (at a cost, of course) the permission to exchange currency or sell sacrificial animals. Since those who came to worship were required to pay the authorized dealers, exploitive practices became common. This was particularly hard on the poor, who would have been able to purchase only doves for sacrifice, the cheapest available alternative. Jesus was not only protesting the presence of commercial activity where only religious practices should have prevailed, He was speaking up for those who were finding it increasingly difficult to attend to temple rites because they could not afford to pay the corrupt dealers of temple privileges.

Today, worshippers on Temple Mount are more likely to be distracted by the intense level of security needed to keep the peace than by any

A model of Herod's reconstructed second temple, located at the Israel Museum

commercial activity. Access to the Western Wall is gained only after passing through high-security surveillance. Those who wish to visit Temple
Mount itself must pass through another set of security stations manned by
armed Israeli Defense Force troops and police. Everywhere in the Old City
of Jerusalem, there is the presence of armed soldiers, a constant reminder
that violence happens not infrequently. It is a sad reflection on the very
violent past on Temple Mount often driven by religious zeal. Until the
building of the wall separating Jerusalem from areas of the West Bank,
suicide bombers, who were often very young, threatened Temple Mount
and other parts of Israel.

Any modern monotheist who would perpetrate violence in order to
achieve a religious goal shares a sense of religious self-justification with
the Crusaders who besieged Jerusalem one thousand years ago. Devaluing
human life is not a deep biblical value. Casual contempt for the sanctity of
life is antithetical to everything Jesus stands for. We see this repeatedly in his
ministry: "And Jesus called a little child unto him, and set him in the midst

of them, and said, Verily I say unto you, except ye be converted, and become as little children, ye shall not enter into the kingdom of heaven. Whosoever therefore shall humble himself as this little child, the same is greatest in the kingdom of heaven. And whoso shall receive one such little child in my name receiveth me. But whoso shall offend one of these little ones which believe in me, it were better for him that a millstone were hanged about his neck, and that he were drowned in the depth of the sea. Woe unto the world because of offences! For it must needs be that offences come; but woe to that man by whom the offence cometh! (Matthew 18:2–7).

In the context of children being induced to become suicide martyrs in the cause of political or religious zeal, Jesus's words call us back to embracing the sacred as a pathway forward in Jerusalem. Golda Meir, a former prime minister of Israel who believed peace would eventually come to her country once said that Middle East peace would come only when we all loved our children more than we hated our enemies. Religious faith is at its finest when it places human life over ideology.

Muslim children enjoying a walk about Temple Mount

For thousands of years, people have been coming to Temple Mount as an expression of what they hold sacred and what gives them their highest motivation. Worshippers from all three major monotheist traditions have come here in the name of their faith to do violence to others. Abraham was taught, however, by His living God that an intent to do harm to the young, even in the name of God, should be stopped; an alternative expression of faith is always possible and will be found at hand (see Genesis 22).

Today, perhaps in the spirit of seeking a sacred experience, visitors to Temple Mount can hearken back to the Jewish pilgrimages to the temple festivals held by God's command three times each year in the spring (Passover), summer (Pentecost), and fall (Tabernacles). In Jesus's time, the final leg of these journeys, regardless of where the pilgrim came from, always led to Jerusalem. Pilgrims literally climbed the south steps of the Temple Mount after enjoying a ritual cleansing bath, perhaps at the Pool of Siloam, just down the hill.

Pilgrims to the temple would sing fifteen psalms, one for each of the final steps into the courts of the temple. These fifteen Psalms (numbers 120 through 134 in the King James Version of the Bible) are known as Songs of Ascent. They are generally cheerful, and all are hopeful. Several of these psalms use the visual imagery of Jerusalem itself to find encouragement for the believer: "As the mountains are round about Jerusalem, so the Lord is round about his people from henceforth even for ever" (Psalms 125:2).

Others of these Songs of Ascent remind the pilgrim of the blessings of the temple, the house of God: "Behold, bless ye the Lord, all ye servants of the Lord, which by night stand in the house of the Lord. Lift up your hands in the sanctuary, and bless the Lord. The Lord that made heaven and earth bless thee out of Zion (Psalms 134:1–3).

Ultimately, the message of these Psalms is that the Abrahamic blessing is for all people to enjoy together. Using a reference to Mount Hermon (remember Har Habtarim, where Abraham received the covenant after arriving in the land of Canaan), the 133 Psalm encourages all of us to remember that what we do matters to us and to God. We have choices, and

The Dome of the Rock

The south wall of Temple Mount with the ancient Southern Steps still intact below

God cares what we do with our moral agency. Let us choose to love one another and embrace our moment on the earth as an opportunity to bless our brothers and sisters, who are God's sons and daughters: "Behold, how good and how pleasant it is for brethren to dwell together in unity! It is like the precious ointment upon the head, that ran down upon the beard, even Aaron's beard: that went down to the skirts of his garments; as the dew of Hermon, and as the dew that descended upon the mountains of Zion: for there the Lord commanded the blessing, even life for evermore" (Psalms 133:1–3).

CHAPTER 4

JERUSALEM OF THE OLD
TESTAMENT PROPHETS

It can be argued that Samuel was the first of Israel's prophets who had no actual ruling function among the tribes. Abraham, Isaac, and Jacob were clan leaders or patriarchs who also served as God's leaders or oracles. Moses clearly led the entire house of Israel, both ecclesiastically and secularly. In fact, his father-in-law, Jethro, a clan leader in his own right, gave Moses instructions about dealing with the tidal wave of temporal matters that naturally comes to the attention of tribal leaders. Evidently, the leadership skills Moses acquired in Pharaoh's administration were more bureaucratic than functional. He needed Jethro's help and insight. Joshua simply stepped into the shoes of Moses after watching him perform for forty years. After Joshua, there was a four-hundred-year interval during which Israelite leaders, called judges, arose to inspire, direct, lead, or otherwise shake up one or more of the twelve tribes. Religious rituals during the era of the judges were conducted at Shiloh, where the ark of the covenant was located in the tabernacle for over three centuries and where a high priest presided over the prescribed festivals and sacrifices.

There is archeological evidence of Shiloh, with several excavations done since 1926. Most recently, objects that might be related to religious worship, including possible tithe offerings, sacrificial animal remains, and a ceramic pomegranate (a fruit motif used as a decoration in Solomon's temple and the high priest's robes).

Today, you can find Shiloh not far from Mount Gerizim, the mountain the Samaritans chose as the place for their temple. A few Samaritans still practice their version of monotheism on Mount Gerizim today.

As the New Testament records, Mount Gerizim looms over Jacob's Well, where Jesus met the Samaritan woman. Today, that site is in Nablus, a Palestinian town in the West Bank to which my Israeli guides have never been able to take me for safety reasons.

Samuel's story begins at Shiloh, where his mother utters the first recorded

Street scene in the Old City of Jerusalem with the ever-present uniformed, armed security troops

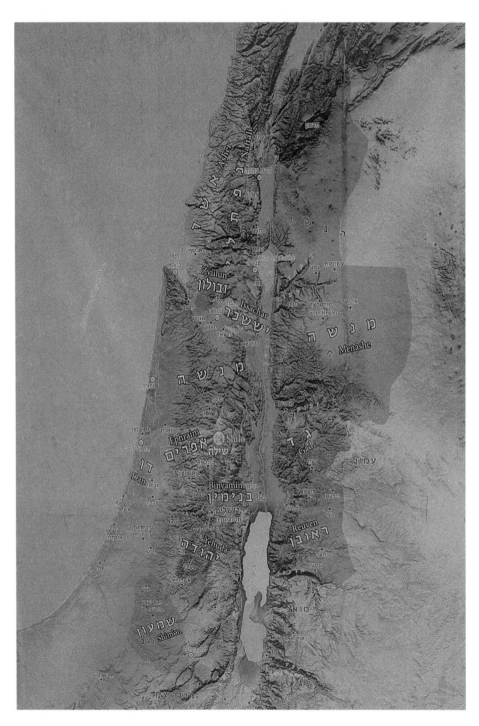

A map of the twelve tribal regions of Israel with the location of Shiloh indicated

personal prayer of biblical record: "So Hannah rose up after they had eaten in Shiloh, and after they had drunk. Now Eli the priest sat upon a seat by a post of the temple of the Lord. And she was in bitterness of soul, and prayed unto the Lord, and wept sore. And she vowed a vow, and said, O Lord of hosts, if thou wilt indeed look on the affliction of thine handmaid,

Modern-day Nablus, where the ancient town of Shechem was located, as seen from Mount Gerizim

Looking down from Mount Gerizim toward Jacob's Well, where Jesus met the Samaritan woman

The hills around ancient Shiloh

and remember me, and not forget thine handmaid, but wilt give unto thine handmaid a man child, then I will give him unto the Lord all the days of his life, and there shall no razor come upon his head. And it came to pass, as she continued praying before the Lord, that Eli marked her mouth. Now Hannah, she spake in her heart; only her lips moved, but her voice was not heard: therefore Eli thought she had been drunken. And Eli said unto her, How long wilt thou be drunken? Put away thy wine from thee. And Hannah answered and said, No, my lord, I am a woman of a sorrowful spirit: I have drunk neither wine nor strong drink, but have poured out my soul before the Lord. Count not thine handmaid for a daughter of Belial: for out of the abundance of my complaint and grief have I spoken hitherto. Then Eli answered and said, Go in peace: and the God of Israel grant thee thy petition that thou hast asked of him. And she said, Let thine handmaid find grace in thy sight. So the woman went her way, and did eat, and her countenance was no more sad" (1 Samuel 1:9–18).

Samuel is born to Hannah in answer to that prayer. He is brought to

The site where the tabernacle and ark of the covenant would have been located at ancient Shiloh

A scene from the modern archeological park at Shiloh

Shiloh, dedicated to the Lord, and brought up as an understudy to Eli, the high priest. It is Eli who helps Samuel recognize the voice of the Lord: "And the child Samuel ministered unto the Lord before Eli. And the word of the Lord was precious in those days; there was no open vision. And it came to pass at that time, when Eli was laid down in his place, and his eyes began to wax dim, that he could not see; and ere the lamp of God went out in the temple of the Lord, where the ark of God was, and Samuel was laid down to sleep; that the Lord called Samuel: and he answered, Here am I. And he ran unto Eli, and said, Here am I; for thou calledst me. And he said, I called not; lie down again. And he went and lay down. And the Lord called yet again, Samuel. And Samuel arose and went to Eli, and said, Here am I; for thou didst call me. And he answered, I called not, my son; lie down again. Now Samuel did not yet know the Lord, neither was the word of the Lord yet revealed unto him. And the Lord called Samuel again the third time. And he arose and went to Eli, and said, Here am I; for thou didst call me. And Eli perceived that the Lord had called the child. Therefore Eli said unto Samuel, Go, lie down: and it shall be, if he call thee, that thou shalt say, Speak, Lord; for thy servant heareth. So Samuel went and lay down in his place. And the Lord came, and stood, and called as at other times, Samuel, Samuel. Then Samuel answered, Speak; for thy servant heareth. And the Lord said to Samuel, Behold, I will do a thing in Israel, at which both the ears of every one that heareth it shall tingle" (1 Samuel 3:1–11).

In addition to receiving attentive training, Samuel was an exceptional and spiritually attuned child. Everyone could see he was prepared to lead in Israel in the tradition of the patriarchs and Moses: "And Samuel grew, and the Lord was with him, and did let none of his words fall to the ground. And all Israel from Dan even to Beer-sheba knew that Samuel was established to be a prophet of the Lord. And the Lord appeared again in Shiloh: for the Lord revealed himself to Samuel in Shiloh by the word of the Lord" (1 Samuel 3:19–21).

Samuel came to the ministry just after the Philistines had defeated Israel and captured the ark of the covenant, which had been taken from Shiloh as if it were a talisman to lead the armies. The news of the defeat and loss of the ark, as well as the death of his sons in battle, proved too much for Samuel's elderly high-priest mentor. Eli fell over backward in his chair and died, leaving the leadership of Israel to Samuel.

The Philistines were an ominous enemy with a local monopoly on iron making, giving them a distinct military advantage over Israel, which explains why Israel, a much more populous nation, had such fear of the Philistines. Samuel's first task as prophet in Israel was to rally his people: "And Samuel spake unto all the house of Israel, saying, If ye do return unto the Lord with all your hearts, then put away the strange gods . . . from among you and prepare your hearts unto the Lord, and serve him only . . . he will deliver you out of the hand of the Philistines. . . . and Samuel cried unto the Lord for Israel; and the Lord heard him. . . . Then Samuel took a stone, and set it between Mizpeh and Shen, and called the name of it Eben-ezer, saying, Hitherto hath the Lord helped us. So the Philistines were subdued, and they came no more into the coast of Israel, and the hand of the Lord was against the Philistines all the days of Samuel" (1 Samuel 7:3, 9–13).

An Ebenezer is a stone of help, or monument, or memorial, to the Lord for the help He has given. Early in his ministry, Samuel already had cause to be grateful for God's help. Over the course of his life, Samuel stayed true to his covenant relationship with God and proved to be both a great spiritual and secular leader in Israel, like Moses and Joshua. But then Samuel's sons, like Eli's sons before, perverted justice and took bribes instead of attending to the people's business properly. This was sufficient cause for the people to demand a new way of ruling in Israel: "Then all the elders of Israel gathered themselves together, and came to Samuel unto Ramah, and said unto him, Behold, thou art old, and thy sons walk not in thy ways: now make us a king to judge us like all the nations" (1 Samuel 8:4–5).

The people of Israel no longer wanted to depend upon the God of Abraham, Isaac, and Jacob to provide a judge or prophet who attended to both temporal affairs, including adjudicating disputes and leading in battle, and spiritual matters. They wanted a social arrangement like other nations had, a king who was full-time dedicated to governance no matter what the cost. Samuel did not think this was a good idea: "But the thing displeased Samuel, when they said, Give us a king to judge us. And Samuel prayed unto the Lord. And the Lord said unto Samuel, Hearken unto the voice of the people in all that they say unto thee: for they have not rejected thee, but they have rejected me, that I should not reign over them" (1 Samuel 8:6–7).

Readers familiar with the Book of Mormon will recall that the Nephites had their own societal discussion about governance and whether it was best done by a king or otherwise. At that point in their history, the Nephites had been blessed by three good kings in Zarahemla: Mosiah, his son Benjamin, and his grandson, also named Mosiah. Mosiah the second, who was the then-current aging monarch, had sons who were eligible to serve as king. None of his sons, however, would accept the duty. Recalling that some Nephites had recently suffered under the rule of a very wicked king named Noah, King Mosiah made the following observations: "Therefore, if it were possible that you could have just men to be your kings, who would establish the laws of God, and judge this people according to his command-ments, yea, if ye could have men for your kings who would do even as my father Benjamin did for this people—I say unto you, if this could always be the case then it would be expedient that ye should always have kings to rule over you. . . . Now I say unto you, that because all men are not just it is not expedient that ye should have a king or kings to rule over you. For behold, how much iniquity doth one wicked king cause to be committed, yea, and what great destruction! Yea, remember king Noah, his wickedness and his abominations, and also the wickedness and abominations of his people. Behold what great destruction did come upon them. . . . And behold, now I say unto you, ye cannot dethrone an iniquitous king save it be through much contention, and the shedding of much blood. For behold, he has his friends in iniquity, and he keepeth his guards about him; and he teareth up the laws of those who have reigned in righteousness before him; and he trampleth under his feet the commandments of God; and he enacteth laws, and sendeth them forth among his people, yea, laws after the manner of his own wickedness; and whosoever doth not obey his laws he causeth to be destroyed; and whosoever doth rebel against him he will send his armies against them to war, and if he can he will destroy them; and thus an unrighteous king doth pervert the ways of all righteousness. And now behold I say unto you, it is not expedient that such abominations should come upon you. Therefore, choose you by the voice of this people, judges, that ye may be judged according to the laws which have been given you by our fathers, which are correct, and which were given them by the hand of the Lord. Now it is not common that the voice of the people desireth anything contrary to that which is right; but it is common for the lesser part of the people to desire that which is not right; therefore this shall ye observe and make it your law—to do your business by the voice of the people. And if the time comes that the voice of the people doth choose iniquity, then is the time that the judgments of God will come upon you;

yea, then is the time he will visit you with great destruction even as he has hitherto visited this land" (Mosiah 29:13–27).

King Mosiah, who would have known the story of the prophet Samuel and King Saul and of the general wickedness of the kings of Judah and Israel, knew from history what Samuel understood from prophecy: it's easy for a despot to despoil a people. King Mosiah anticipated that majority rule had better odds of preventing societal decay than monarchy, but he also knew that majority rule could deteriorate into injustice, inequity, and iniquity. How prescient King Mosiah now seems. Samuel, who didn't have such historical precedents for his people, could only watch as they rejected God's rule for kingly prerogatives.

So Samuel became the first of a new breed of religious leaders in Israel: a prophet without any secular leadership responsibility. To be sure, the new regime had a rocky start. After seeking out and finding the first king, Saul, Samuel had to go looking again when Saul proved unworthy. Samuel had made it clear to Saul that he was a king and, as such, was meant to look after the temporal governance of the house of Israel, while Samuel retained the priestly and spiritual leadership. Saul, however, didn't maintain the separation between religious leadership and his kingly duties. After serving only two years, Saul became impatient waiting for Samuel to arrive in a camp of warriors about to engage the Philistines in battle: "As for Saul, he was yet in Gilgal, and all the people followed him trembling. And he tarried seven days, according to the set time that Samuel had appointed: but Samuel came not to Gilgal; and the people were scattered from him. And Saul said, Bring hither a burnt offering to me, and peace offerings. And he offered the burnt offering. And it came to pass, that as soon as he had made an end of offering the burnt offering, behold, Samuel came; and Saul went out to meet him, that he might salute him. And Samuel said, What hast thou done? And Saul said, Because I saw that the people were scattered from me, and that thou camest not within the days appointed, and that the Philistines gathered themselves together at Michmash; Therefore said I, The Philistines will come down now upon me to

Gilgal, and I have not made supplication unto the Lord: I forced myself therefore, and offered a burnt offering. And Samuel said to Saul, Thou hast done foolishly: thou hast not kept the commandment of the Lord thy God, which he commanded thee" (1 Samuel 13:7–13).

Thus began the very troubled relationship between the men who became kings in Israel and the prophets who spoke for God to the children of Abraham, Isaac, and Jacob. After repeatedly disobeying the Lord's commandments, as articulated by Samuel, Saul was rejected as king: "Then came the word of the Lord unto Samuel, saying, It repenteth me that I have set up Saul to be king: for he is turned back from following me, and hath not performed my commandments. And it grieved Samuel; and he cried unto the Lord all night. And Samuel said, Behold, to obey is better than sacrifice, and to hearken than the fat of rams. Because thou hast rejected the word of the Lord, he hath also rejected thee from being king. And Saul said unto Samuel, I have sinned: for I have transgressed the commandment of the Lord, and thy words: because I feared the people, and obeyed their

The theater at Beth Shan

The ruins of Beth Shan

The hill where the pagan temple was located in the Roman town at Beth Shan

voice. Now therefore, I pray thee, pardon my sin, and turn again with me, that I may worship the Lord. And Samuel said unto Saul, I will not return with thee: for thou hast rejected the word of the Lord [who] hath rent the kingdom of Israel from thee this day. . . . Then Samuel went to Ramah; and Saul went up to his house to Gibeah of Saul. And Samuel came no more to see Saul until the day of his death: nevertheless Samuel mourned for Saul: and the Lord repented that he had made Saul king over Israel" (1 Samuel 15:1–35).

Before he died, Samuel anointed another king in Israel: David. For his part, while he sought to kill David, Saul never gave up wanting to rekindle his relationship of trust with God and his prophet Samuel, but he was never able to fully understand that it required a complete commitment and humble obedience to God's commandments. Saul persisted in trying to do things his way. On the night before his final battle with the Philistines, Saul sought to have Samuel renew God's interest in Saul's cause by calling to Samuel from beyond the grave using the services of a woman with a "familiar spirit"; in other words, he asked a medium to hold a séance. Samuel did appear to Saul but provided no comfort to him and instead issued a prediction of Israel's defeat and Saul's death. The next day was disastrous for the armies of Israel, and Saul and his sons were killed, their bodies hung on the city walls of Beth-shan. (Beth-shan is now a remarkable archeological site—perhaps the best ruin of a Roman city available to tourists.)

A TIME OF TURMOIL

During Samuel's lifetime, Jerusalem remained in the hands of the Jebusites, one of the Canaanite tribes not driven out by Joshua. After Samuel's death and that of Saul, David's anointing as king was ratified by the entire nation of Israel, and among the first tasks he set for himself was the conquering of the Jebusite city that became Jerusalem, which was designated by King David as the capital city of his empire.

As the capital of first the combined kingdom of all twelve tribes and later that of the kingdom of Judah (the Southern Kingdom) after the civil war that divided Israel after King Solomon's death, Jerusalem was the stage for much of the ongoing tension between the kings of Israel and the prophets of God. Most of the kings were flawed men who pursued their own interests and not those of God or His chosen people. In fact, all the kings of the Northern Kingdom were like Ahab, who was uninterested in righteousness and put a price on the prophet Elijah's head. As king of Northern Israel, Ahab never ruled in Jerusalem. But with only a couple of noteworthy exceptions, the kings in Jerusalem who ruled over the kingdom of Judah were just as evil as Ahab.

After conquering the Jebusite city, David built a walled city to the south of Mount Moriah, eventually buying Mount Moriah and designating it as the then-future building site of the temple, a task he left to his son Solomon.

The area where David built his palace is now an active archeological site

The area representing the City of David in the first-century-AD Jerusalem model at the Israel Museum

known as the City of David, which is located outside and to the south of the Ottoman-built walls of the Old City of Jerusalem. Biblical minimalists, including leading Muslim community members, do not accept that there was a regionally dominant Hebrew kingdom during the Iron Age (tenth to ninth centuries BC). Kings David and Solomon are key figures in Jewish history according to the Old Testament, and proving their historicity is vital to establishing the ongoing claim that Jerusalem was originally founded by the Jews, who also built the temple, making it the religious center of Judaism. Denial of the existence of a regime capable of carrying out massive construction projects is central to the purposes of those whose intent is to deny Judaism any primal claim either on the actual territory or the origins of monotheism. Christians, because Jesus is said in the New Testament to be the heir to David's throne, have tended to support Jewish claims about the artifacts discovered through archeological methods in the City of David.

Hezekiah

A few kings who sat upon the Davidic throne had better relationships with the prophets who served God than did Saul with Samuel. One such king was Hezekiah, who lived in Jerusalem nearly three thousand years ago. It is said that "he trusted in the Lord God of Israel . . . for he clave to the Lord, and departed not from following him, but kept his commandments, which the Lord commanded Moses. And the Lord was with him; and he prospered whithersoever he went forth" (2 Kings 18:5–7).

Hezekiah was twenty-five years old when he came to the throne in Jerusalem. During his reign as King of Judah, the Northern Kingdom of Israel was conquered by the Assyrian army, and the ten tribes were taken forever from their homeland. But the kingdom of Judah was preserved because Hezekiah "did that which was right in the sight of the Lord, . . . trusted in the Lord God of Israel . . . for he clave to the Lord, and departed not from following him . . . and the Lord was with him" (2 Kings 18:2–3, 5–7). At age forty, Hezekiah came down with a mortal illness.

The prophet Isaiah came to Hezekiah and declared: "Set thine house in order: for thou shalt die, and not live. Then Hezekiah turned his face toward the wall, and prayed unto the Lord, and said, Remember now, O Lord, I beseech thee, how I have walked before thee in truth and with a perfect heart, and have done that which is good in thy sight. And Hezekiah wept sore." Under direction from God, Isaiah returned to Hezekiah and said: "I have heard thy prayer, I have seen thy tears: behold, I will add unto thy days fifteen years" (Isaiah 38:1–5).

Despite the major distractions in his life, Hezekiah stayed on the Lord's errand. He opened the temple, removed the pagan shrines his predecessor had placed there, reconsecrated the sanctuary, and reorganized the Levites and priests. He taught his people to honor their covenants, saying: "Ye children of Israel, turn again unto the Lord God of Abraham, Isaac, and Israel, and he will return to . . . you . . . and be not ye like your fathers . . . but yield yourselves unto the Lord, and enter into his sanctuary . . . and serve the Lord your God" (2 Chronicles 30:6–8).

To this day, one can see Hezekiah's wall in the Jewish Quarter of Old Jerusalem, built to expand the city walls and make room for refugees from the Northern Kingdom after its defeat by the Assyrians.

I believe it likely that Lehi's grandparents were among those refugees, as Lehi's tribe, Manasseh, was from the north. And you can walk the

Ruins of Hezekiah's wall in Old Jerusalem

length of Hezekiah's tunnel, which was built to bring the water of the Gihon Spring inside the city walls for survival during the Assyrian siege, as well as a means to hinder the enemy force by denying them a water source. These are monuments to a man who led his people on the Lord's errand by yielding himself to God.

PROPHETS OF ANCIENT ISRAEL

You can think of the prophets of ancient Israel as God's servants who lived their lives during the two major movements of the house of Israel documented in the Old Testament. Moses was the sole prophet of the Exodus from Egypt, the first such major movement. His story is well documented in the first five books of the Old Testament and generally understood by all people, even those who have a rudimentary familiarity with the Old Testament. The second major movement of Israel, however, known as the scattering of Israel, is less well understood, in part because it occurred over a time frame of about two centuries.

There are many prophets whose writings include information about the scattering of Israel. Moses lived about 1300 BC. The prophets of the scattering lived years later, between 800 BC and about 400 BC. These prophets spoke and wrote extensively about the scattering of Israel, which they prophesied would be the consequence of the wickedness of the people of Israel, both in the Northern Kingdom (the kingdom of Israel, where the ten tribes lived) and in the Southern Kingdom (the kingdom of Judah, where the tribe of Judah dominated, along with the tribe of Benjamin, including Jerusalem and the temple of Solomon). These prophets were disturbed about what they were inspired to say to their brothers and sisters in Israel. They feared the special covenants between Israel and the Lord might be forever lost because of the people's disregard of God's laws. They themselves sought reassurance from the Lord about the preservation of these special covenants and the restoration of Israel.

Amos

One of the first of these prophets, Amos, lived and served God in the Northern Kingdom before its destruction in about 750 BC. A contemporary of Isaiah (who lived in the kingdom of Judah), Amos made it clear that through His prophets, the Lord was revealing everything pertinent to the scattering of Israel: "Surely the Lord God will do nothing but he revealeth his secret unto his servants the prophets" (Amos 3:7).

But the Lord also revealed through these same prophets many important secrets about the restoration of Israel. These instructions, intended to give hope and guidance to those who followed the covenant, are also very important today for those living in the time of the gathering of Israel, because God intends all people to eventually make a decision about whether they will follow Him or not, with serious consequences attached to that choice.

About the scattering of Israel, Amos said, "Woe to them that are at ease in Zion, and trust in the mountain of Samaria. . . . Therefore now shall they go captive. . . . The Lord God hath sworn by himself, saith the Lord God of hosts, I abhor the excellency of Jacob, and hate his palaces: therefore will I deliver up the city with all that is therein. . . . But, behold, I will raise up against you a nation, O house of Israel, saith the Lord the God of hosts; and they shall afflict you" (Amos 6:1, 7–8, 14).

The nation raised up against the kingdom of Israel was Assyria, with its capital in Nineveh, the city Jonah brought to repentance. Like all ancient conquering nations, Assyria was not able to sustain itself and eventually fell to Babylon, a neighboring nation. For most of ancient history (up to about 300 BC), Babylon, with a population of around two hundred thousand, was the largest city in the world. A probable location of the Tower of Babel, it was located on the Euphrates River about 50 miles south of what is modern-day Baghdad in Iraq. Two of the seven wonders of the ancient world were in Babylon. The first was the city wall, which was 56 miles long and 300 feet high, with a 35-feet underground extension. The wall had 250 towers, each 450 feet high. A second wall was located 75 feet inside the first. The two walls were surrounded by a moat that was 250 feet across. Each of the eight city gates was a massive double structure (one for each of the walls) covered in hundreds of beautiful raised-relief figures. Two of the lions at the Ishtar gate can be seen in New York City's Metropolitan Museum of Art, and the smaller of the two parts of the Ishtar gate has been reconstructed in a museum in Berlin, Germany. The wall and its gates were truly a wonder.

The second wonder of the city of Babylon was the Hanging Gardens. These were built on stilts 75 feet above street level and irrigated hydraulically using water from the Euphrates. King Nebuchadnezzar, ruler of Babylon during the time of the conquest of the kingdom of Judah (about 680 BC), created in the Hanging Gardens a mountain rainforest inside an arid city. The streets of the city were paved with three-feet-square stone slabs. There were two massive golden images in the middle of the city, one of the god Baal and the other of a table. Each of these images weighed 50,000 pounds and would be worth $1.3 billion each given today's gold prices. In the midst of this was the great tower—probably built on the site of the Tower of Babel and called "House of the Platform of Heaven"—which was 300 feet high and topped by a temple to the local god. Nebuchadnezzar's Palace was said to be unequaled in all human history.

The prophets of the scattering—Jeremiah, Ezekiel, Daniel, Lehi, Nephi, Nahum, Zephaniah, Obadiah, and Habakkuk—were all living and prophesying just before or during the time of the Babylonian invasion of Jerusalem.

The king of Judah, Zedekiah, was captured and forced to watch all but one of his sons executed. (The Book of Mormon records that one of his sons, Mulek, escaped this fate and brought a group of people to the Americas, later joining the Nephites.) After Zedekiah watched his sons' executions, he was blinded and brought captive to Babylon with most of the remnant of the Jews who had been living in Jerusalem.

Ezekiel

Ezekiel, who had been serving among the priests of the temple, was part of the fraction of those captured and enslaved and probably served on the massive public-works projects that made the wonders of Babylon. Daniel, who was of royal blood, was brought into Nebuchadnezzar's protection and trained up to be useful to the royal house of Babylon.

As all of this occurred, the people of Israel wondered if they and their covenants with God would even survive this catastrophe. Ezekiel voiced this concern: "Then fell I down upon my face, and cried with a loud voice, and said, Ah Lord God! wilt thou make a full end of the remnant of Israel? Again the word of the Lord came unto me, saying, Son of man, thy brethren, even thy brethren, the men of thy kindred, and all the house of Israel wholly, are they unto whom the inhabitants of Jerusalem have said, Get you far from the Lord: unto us is this land given in possession. Therefore say, Thus saith the Lord God; although I have cast them far off among the heathen, and although I have scattered them among the countries, yet will I be to them as a little sanctuary in the countries where they shall come. Therefore say, Thus saith the Lord God; I will even gather you from the people, and assemble you out of the countries where ye have been scattered, and I will give you the land of Israel. And they shall come thither, and they shall take away all the detestable things thereof and all the abominations thereof from thence. And I will give them one heart, and I will put a new spirit within you; and I will take the stony heart out of their flesh, and will give them an heart of flesh: that they may walk in my statutes, and keep mine ordinances, and do them: and they shall be my people, and I will be their God" (Ezekiel 11:13-20).

Note that in this passage, Ezekiel prophecies three things: 1) the inhabitants of Jerusalem, clearly at some future date, will claim that God has given them the land of Jerusalem for possession and they will deny that "the house of Israel," who are the kindred of Ezekiel, have any right to live there; 2) in response, God promises that throughout a prolonged absence from the land of Jerusalem during which the house of Israel will dwell "among the heathen" scattered in many countries, the people of Israel will maintain their identity as God's people because God will arrange to serve as a sanctuary for them; and 3) at some point, God will act to gather His people and give them the land of Jerusalem again. As they gather back to their land, the house of Israel will remove "detestable things" and "abominations" (they will abandon the wickedness of worldly philosophies and practices), and God will give them one heart so they can walk in His statutes, keep his ordinances, and once again be the people of God.

This was the concise formula given by the ancient prophets of Israel for the gathering of Israel in the latter days, our days: repent of your sins, get a new heart committed to God, love God with all your heart, keep God's commandments, and enter into covenants with Him. The same formula applies to every one of God's children who desires to partake of His promised blessings, no matter what trials they currently face or culture they live in.

Daniel

While Ezekiel is preaching this formula for renewing the covenant of Israel and predicting a time when the gathering shall come to pass, Daniel is helping King Nebuchadnezzar at the palace. The king has had a recurring dream. Though it troubles him greatly, he cannot remember the dream. He summons his wise men, but they are unable to help him. They promise to interpret the dream if the king will tell them what the dream is about, but since he cannot remember the dream, all are frustrated, and Nebuchadnezzar threatens to execute the wise men for being unable to help him with his dream.

Into this threatening situation steps Daniel. He and his Jewish friends pray for divine intervention, and Daniel reports to the king: "Thou, O king, sawest and behold a great image. This great image, whose brightness was excellent, stood before thee; and the form thereof was terrible. This image's head was of fine gold, his breast and his arms of silver, his belly and his thighs of brass, his legs of iron, his feet part of iron and part of clay. Thou sawest till that a stone was cut out without hands, which smote the image upon his feet that were of iron and clay, and brake them to pieces. Then was the iron, the clay, the brass, the silver, and the gold, broken to pieces together, and became like the chaff of the summer threshingfloors; and the wind carried them away, that no place was found for them; and the stone that smote the image became a great mountain and filled the whole earth" (Daniel 2:31–35).

Once Daniel has vividly described Nebuchadnezzar's dream, he goes on to explain what it means: "And in the days of these kings shall the God of heaven set up a kingdom, which shall never be destroyed: and the kingdom shall not be left to other people, but it shall break in pieces and consume all these kingdoms, and it shall stand forever. Forasmuch as thou sawest the stone was cut out of the mountain without hands, and that it brake in pieces the iron, the brass, the clay, the silver, and the gold; the great God hath made known to the king what shall come to pass hereafter: and the dream is certain, and the interpretation thereof sure" (Daniel 2:44–45).

BECOMING PARTICIPANTS IN THE GATHERING OF ISRAEL

Ezekiel and Daniel, both in Babylon, clearly prophesied a remarkable future event: the gathering of Israel and the establishment of the kingdom of God on earth. As big and marvelous as was Babylon, what they saw in the future was much bigger and much better, and, from an eternal perspective, much more important. These prophets, who were forced to watch the demise of their beloved Jerusalem and their temple demolished had every reason to want to know whether and how the people of Israel would ever enjoy God's blessings again. They were shown the events in our day that would reestablish Israel, down to the details about how we, the children of Israel in the latter days, could participate in that great gathering. Here is what they taught:

1. Be like Daniel—do not defile yourself with the temptations of Babylon but be obedient. Daniel was brought to that fabulous city Babylon and placed in the royal household. He was commanded to participate in the elite preparatory school for the highest level of administrative and diplomatic service to the throne, down to the regimen of diet and exercise. He could have been dazzled by Babylon and this opportunity. Daniel instead adhered to what he had been taught in Jerusalem. For instance, when Daniel and his companions were selected to be educated and trained in the royal court, they were offered rich foods (meat and wine) by the king's servants. Instead of eating the rich foods and wine the king provided, Daniel and his companions kept themselves undefiled by eating pulses and water and proved to be healthier and more alert.

2. Be like Daniel and perform your religious observances carefully and consistently. Later in Daniel's career, Darius was king in Babylon. The king was persuaded to issue a command that no one could pray to anyone other than him. Daniel knew that the penalty for disobedience to this rule was death, but he said his personal prayers nonetheless. Darius was forced to have Daniel committed to the lion's den overnight and was very pleased when Daniel emerged unscathed the next morning.

3. Don't be like Jonah, who disobeyed the commandment of the Lord. He was called on a mission to the Assyrian city of Nineveh to preach repentance, but he refused and fled to Tarshish (modern-day Spain). Almost everyone knows the story of how the Lord arranged to have him returned to fulfill his mission, which he did very unwillingly (it took quite a storm and being swallowed by a whale to convince him) because he was biased against the Assyrians. Upon hearing his preaching, the people of Nineveh

repented, perhaps setting them up to eventually be the nation that later defeated the Northern Kingdom and scattered the ten tribes of Israel. Jonah's reaction to his success as a prophet in Nineveh is remarkably rebellious: "But it displeased Jonah exceedingly, and he was very angry. And he prayed unto the Lord, and said, I pray thee, O Lord, was not this my saying, when I was yet in my country? Therefore I fled before unto Tarshish: for I knew that thou are a gracious God, and merciful, slow to anger, and of great kindness, and repentest thee of the evil. Therefore now, O Lord, take, I beseech thee, my life from me; for it is better for me to die than to live" (Jonah 4:1–3).

Jonah knew going into his preaching that the Assyrians might repent and that if they did, the Lord in His goodness would change His intent and spare that nation. And Jonah wanted no part of sparing them. He obviously disliked the Assyrians, so much so that he asked to have his own life taken when the Lord spared the city of Nineveh. There is no room in the gathering of Israel for anyone with Jonah's nationalistic feelings. And there is a further lesson: what we do when preaching has potential powerful effects both on the people who listen to us and perhaps on God, who might well change His purposes to accommodate those who repent.

4. Instead of Jonah's foolish example, follow instead Zechariah's counsel. Zechariah lived nearly a century after Daniel and Ezekiel in the time when a small number of Jews were allowed to return from Babylon to Jerusalem and rebuild the temple. Zechariah knew his return to Jerusalem was not the great gathering of Israel foretold by Daniel and Ezekiel. Rather, he called his time the "day of small things." It was important for him to reestablish a Jewish presence and temple in Jerusalem as the backdrop for the life and ministry of Jesus Christ, but Zechariah knew that a great gathering would happen in the latter days. And he advises us in our day as follows: "These are the things that ye shall do; speak ye every man the truth

to his neighbour; execute the judgment of truth and peace in your gates: and let none of you imagine evil in your hearts against his neighbor; and love no false oath: for all these things I hate, saith the Lord. . . . Thus saith the Lord of Hosts; in those days it come to pass that ten men shall take hold . . . of [your] skirt saying, We will go with you: for we have heard that God is with you" (Zechariah 8:16–23). Why will people follow your spiritual lead in these times of gathering? Because you are honest with them and fair to them and you give them the benefit of the doubt by judging them and their works in good faith.

5. Embrace the Book of Mormon, as prophesied by Ezekiel: "The word of the Lord came again unto me, saying, moreover thou son of man, take thee one stick and write upon it, for Judah, and for the children of Israel his companions: then take another stick, and write upon it, for Joseph, the stick of Ephraim, and for all the house of Israel his companions: and join them one to another into one stick; and they shall become one in thine hand. And when the children of thy people shall speak unto thee, saying, Wilt thou not shew us what thou meanest by these? Say unto them, Thus saith the Lord God; Behold, I will take the stick of Joseph, which is in the hand of Ephraim, and the tribes of Israel his fellows, and will put them with him, even with the stick of Judah, and make them one stick, and they shall be one in mine hand. And the sticks whereon thou writest shall be in thine hand before their eyes. And say unto them, Thus saith the Lord God; Behold, I will take the children of Israel from among the heathen, whither they be gone, and will gather them on every side, and bring them into their own land" (Ezekiel 37:15–23). If you wish to participate in the gathering of Israel, base your actions, choices, and preaching on the scriptures of Judah and Joseph.

6. Ezekiel, who had officiated at the temple in Jerusalem, not surprisingly cared a great deal about the reestablishment of the temple

during the gathering. He prophesied that the sanctuary of the Lord would again be established in the days of the gathering. "Moreover I will make a covenant of peace with them; it shall be an everlasting covenant with them: and I will place them, and multiply them, and will set my sanctuary in the midst of them forevermore. My tabernacle also shall be with them: yea, I will be their God, and they shall be my people. And the heathen shall know that I the Lord do sanctify Israel, when my sanctuary shall be in the midst of them forevermore" (Ezekiel 37:26–28). Temple work is the work of sanctification. Be in the temple if you want to be prepared to assist in the gathering of Israel.

7. Honor the priesthood as taught by Malachi. Malachi, the last prophet whose writings are included in the Old Testament, lived in Jerusalem about four hundred years before Christ. He knew the history of the demise of the Northern Kingdom and the capture of Jerusalem by the Babylonians. He was part of the remnant of Jews whose forefathers had returned from Babylon to Jerusalem to build the second temple. From his unique vantage point in history, Malachi foresaw the need for the sealing power to be restored to the earth and knew that Elijah would serve that restoring function. Though ancient Israel (because it had rejected the fullness of the gospel offered by God through Moses at Mount Sinai) knew only limited priesthood service through the tribe of Levi, Malachi anticipated the restoration of all things by teaching that God "hath been witness between thee and the wife of thy youth" and that "she is thy companion, and the wife of thy covenant" (Malachi 2:14). In the context of the shared priesthood commitments of men and women, Malachi teaches that "the priest's lips should keep knowledge, and they should seek the law at his mouth: for he is the messenger of the Lord of hosts" (Malachi 2:7). When we accept the oath and covenant of the priesthood, we promise to live such that we can be a messenger of God to His people.

8. If we are obedient like Daniel, honest and open with our neighbors like Zechariah, embrace the Book of Mormon and the temple as taught by Ezekiel, and honor the priesthood as directed by Malachi—we will enjoy the great blessing of the Spirit which the prophet Joel saw coming in our day and which was reiterated by the angel Moroni to Joseph Smith: "And it shall come to pass afterward that I will pour out my spirit upon all flesh; and your sons and your daughters shall prophesy, your old men shall dream dreams, your young men shall see visions: and also upon the servants and upon the handmaids in those days will I pour out my spirit. And it shall come to pass, that whosoever shall call on the name of the Lord shall be delivered: for in Mount Zion and in Jerusalem shall be deliverance, as the Lord hath said, and in the remnant whom the Lord shall call" (Joel 2:28–32). Those who would serve the Lord in the gathering of Israel will need the gift of the Spirit to confirm their calling and prepare them for the rigors of serving the Lord.

9. Ezekiel had exactly this kind of outpouring of the Spirit when he received his call to serve the Lord as a prophet in Babylon: "And he said unto me, Son of man, stand upon thy feet, and I will speak unto thee. And the spirit entered into me when he spake unto me, and set me upon my feet, that I heard him that spake unto me. And he said unto me, Son of man, I send thee to the children of Israel, to a rebellious nation that hath rebelled against me, even unto this very day. For they are impudent children and stiffhearted. I do send thee unto them; and thou shalt say unto them, thus saith the Lord God. And they, whether they will hear, or whether they will forbear . . . yet shall know that there hath been a prophet among them" (Ezekiel 2:1–5). We will need the Spirit because the prophet Zephaniah prophesied that in our day we would be surrounded by practical atheists who "say in their heart, the Lord will not do good, neither will he do evil" (Zephaniah 1:12). Most Americans

believe in God, but many do not believe God will actually act in their lives. They are practical atheists.

10. What we need from the Spirit is to be changed in our hearts, or transformed and converted unto the Lord, like Jeremiah, whose ministry lasted forty years during the most wicked times in Jerusalem just before and during the Babylonian invasion. Jeremiah was beaten, put in the stocks, often imprisoned in deplorable confinements, and eventually kidnapped and murdered. Despite this persecution, he never wavered from the cause of the Lord. During one of his imprisonments, he said, "The Lord's word was in mine heart as a burning fire shut up in my bones, and I was weary with forbearing, and I could not stay. But the Lord is with me as a mighty terrible one: therefore my persecutors shall stumble and they shall not prevail" (Jeremiah 20:9).

We must live like Old Testament prophets if we are to do the work of gathering they foresaw in our day. If we do, we will have the mighty change of heart they saw for the righteous in the latter days: "Behold the days come, saith the Lord, that I will make a new covenant with the house of Israel, and with the house of Judah: not according to the covenant that I made with their fathers in the day that I took them by the hand to bring them out of the land of Egypt; which my covenant they brake, although I was an husband unto them, saith the Lord: but this shall be the covenant that I will make with the house of Israel: after those days, saith the Lord, I will put my law in their inward parts, and write it in their hearts; and will be their God, and they shall be my people" (Jeremiah 31:31–33).

11. Zechariah sums up the need for action in this day of gathering: "I will strengthen the house of Judah, and I will save the house of Joseph, and I will bring them again to place them; for I have mercy upon them: and they shall be as though I had not cast them off: for I am the Lord their God, and will hear them. And they of Ephraim

shall be like a mighty man, and their heart shall rejoice . . . yea, their children shall see it, and be glad; their heart shall rejoice in the Lord. I will hiss for them, and gather them; for I have redeemed them: and they shall increase as they have increased. And I will sow them among the people: and they shall remember me in far countries; and they shall live with their children, and turn again. I will bring them again also out of the land of Egypt, and gather them out of Assyria. . . . and I will strengthen them in the Lord; and they shall walk up and down in his name, saith the Lord" (Zechariah 10:6–12).

It is time we walked up and down in the name of the Lord. We live in a society of practical atheists, surrounded by the dazzling beauties and iniquities of Babylon. Yet the Lord has promised He will gather His people and bless them. The ancient prophets of Israel saw our day and knew that many of us would directly participate in the literal gathering of Israel and the establishment of the kingdom of God on the earth. They rejoiced in our day because it gave them assurance that Jerusalem and the temple they had seen destroyed would one day be restored.

CHAPTER 5

THE PASSION OF CHRIST

Both the compilation of Old Testament prophecy just summarized and the prophetic statements ascribed to Jesus Christ in the New Testament are discounted by biblical minimalists. It is a fact of history that Jerusalem was destroyed by a pagan army not long after Jesus died. As a part of that destruction, the second temple, as it had been remarkably expanded and restored by King Herod the Great, was burned and its remnants taken down with not one stone left upon another, as foretold by Jesus. Jesus also prophesied of His own death and Resurrection.

Biblical minimalists allege that after Jesus died, these statements were fabricated by His adherents, who gradually built a belief system around Jesus that went far beyond what He had said of Himself while He was alive. These naysaying scholars insist it would have been easy for Jesus's followers to have written "prophecies" about the downfall of Jerusalem after it happened in 70 AD (or CE, as it is now known, in order to refrain from references to Jesus Christ in dating customs).

As for the Resurrection, they feel that no effort is required to discredit the New Testament account since people can't rise from the dead, at least in usual experience. Never mind that many eyewitnesses to the Resurrection are identified or that a number of these immediately began testifying of what they saw. There was no protracted period of oral tradition leading to a later generation of the Resurrection story. It is historical fact that the followers of Jesus who personally knew Him were prepared to suffer death rather than retract their witness that He rose from the dead.

For Christians, Jesus Christ is the ultimate prophetic voice associated with Jerusalem. According to the Gospels of Matthew and Luke, He was born in Bethlehem because He was the heir to the throne of David. If Israel had not fallen out of favor with God and created the conditions that led to its conquest, first by the Assyrians in the north and then by the Babylonians overcoming the kingdom of Judah in the south, the house of David would have continued to rule and Jesus would have been king, uniting the prophetic office with the secular governance, as had last been the case when Samuel was the prophet in Israel.

Jesus was well aware of that history. He knew that the failings of Israel throughout its history had led to a recurring need for prophetic voices calling for repentance, and that remained so in His own lifetime. Jesus knew that the sins of the people of Israel put Jerusalem in peril. He made several statements about this:

> Nevertheless I must walk to day, and to morrow, and the day following: for it cannot be that a prophet perish out of Jerusalem. O Jerusalem, Jerusalem, which killest the prophets, and stonest them that are sent unto thee; how often would I have gathered thy children together, as a hen doth gather her brood under her wings, and ye would not! Behold, your house is left unto you desolate: and verily I say unto you, Ye shall not see me, until the time come when ye shall say, Blessed is he that cometh in the name of the Lord. (Luke 13:33–35)

Woe unto you! for ye build the sepulchres of the prophets, and your fathers killed them. Truly ye bear witness that ye allow the deeds of your fathers: for they indeed killed them, and ye build their sepulchres. Therefore also said the wisdom of God, I will send them prophets and apostles, and some of them they shall slay and persecute: that the blood of all the prophets, which was shed from the foundation of the world, may be required of this generation. (Luke 11:47–50)

And as he went out of the temple, one of his disciples saith unto him, Master, see what manner of stones and what buildings are here! And Jesus answering said unto him, Seest thou these great buildings? There shall not be left one stone upon another, that shall not be thrown down. (Mark 13:1–2)

But when ye shall see the abomination of desolation, spoken of by Daniel the prophet, standing where it ought not, (let him that readeth understand,) then let them that be in Judæa flee to the mountains: and let him that is on the housetop not go down into the house, neither enter therein, to take any thing out of his house: and let him that is in the field not turn back again for to take up his garment. But woe to them that are with child, and to them that give suck in those days! And pray ye that your flight be not in the winter. For in those days shall be affliction, such as was not from the beginning of the creation which God created unto this time, neither shall be. (Mark 13:14–19)

Jesus was clearly forecasting that Jerusalem would be the stage for His penultimate act of sacrifice. This is why Zechariah prophesied that in his own day, the "day of small things," the people of Israel were to come back to Jerusalem to rebuild the city and temple not because these efforts to rebuild were to be permanent but because the Messiah must live out His mortal life and be killed amongst the house of Israel and in its home territory. Jesus, the ultimate prophet, must be misunderstood and mistreated, persecuted and killed in Jerusalem, as prophets had been many times before. As a consequence, the city of Jerusalem, its temple, and its people would be left desolate. And a Gentile nation would once again erect a pagan structure on Temple Mount (the abomination of desolation Daniel had predicted, which had previously occurred under Greek rule in the second century BC).

Like the prophets before Him, Jesus prophesied that after His own suffering and death, the people of Israel would be scattered by force from Jerusalem until a future time of gathering: "And when ye shall see Jerusalem compassed with armies, then know that the desolation thereof is nigh. Then let them which are in Judæa flee to the mountains; and let them which are in the midst of it depart out; and let not them that are in the countries enter thereinto. For these be the days of vengeance, that all things which are written may be fulfilled. But woe unto them that are with child, and to them that give suck, in those days! For there shall be great distress in the land, and wrath upon this people. And they shall fall by the edge of the sword, and shall be led away captive into all nations: and Jerusalem shall be trodden down of the Gentiles, until the times of the Gentiles be fulfilled" (Luke 21:20–24).

BETHANY

The week of His passion began on a Sunday. It had only been a short time since Jesus had been in Bethany, a town just on the other side of the Mount of Olives from Jerusalem. He had come at the bidding of Mary and Martha to heal their brother Lazarus from a mortal illness. John, his Gospel being the sole source of information about this episode, infers that Jesus, having received the urgent summons from the two sisters, intentionally delayed His arrival in Bethany until after Lazarus died. Jesus had raised others from the dead before, but this episode specifically mentions how Lazarus had been deceased for four days in order for the reader to know that Lazarus really was dead and couldn't have been just revived from a swoon or coma. Speaking to Martha just before He raised Lazarus from the dead, Jesus pronounced perhaps most clearly the doctrine of Resurrection: "Jesus said unto her, I am the resurrection, and the life: he that believeth in me, though he were dead, yet shall he live: and whosoever liveth and believeth in me shall never die. Believest thou this?" (John 11: 25–6).

Whether we believe in the literal, physical Resurrection of Jesus or not is increasingly a key to whether we are really Christian or not. Biblical minimalists can also be self-described monotheists, like Muslims who state that God has no son, or Christians who accept the Resurrection as a metaphorical event. A true disciple of Christ doesn't follow a feel-good myth but the real Savior of the world.

PALM SUNDAY

On that Sunday before Passover, the average citizen of Jerusalem was in great anticipation about whether Jesus of Nazareth would come to the Passover Feast. What had happened with Lazarus just days before was well known. That Jesus had not attended the Feast of Tabernacles the previous fall was probably also known. But likely also known was the fact that the chief priest had decided to arrange for deaths of Jesus and Lazarus: "Then gathered the chief priests and the Pharisees a council, and said, What do we? for this man doeth many miracles. If we let him thus alone, all men will believe on him: and the Romans shall come and take away both our place and nation. And one of them, named Caiaphas, being the high priest that same year, said unto them, Ye know nothing at all, nor consider that it is expedient for us, that one man should die for the people, and that the whole nation perish not. And this spake he not of himself: but being high priest that year, he prophesied that Jesus should die for that nation; and not for that nation only, but that also he should gather together in one the children of God that were scattered abroad. Then from that day forth they took counsel together for to put him to death" (John 11:47–53).

While many people believed in Jesus and would have gladly welcomed Him to Jerusalem, many more were probably glad for the spectacle and public conflict His coming to Jerusalem was likely to generate. Zechariah, the prophet of the day of small things in Jerusalem, foresaw the celebration that would arise upon the Savior's entry into the city: "Rejoice greatly, O daughter of Zion; shout, O daughter of Jerusalem: behold, thy King cometh unto thee: he is just, and having salvation; lowly, and riding upon an ass, and upon a colt the foal of an ass" (Zechariah 9:9).

The Palm Sunday celebration is recounted in all four Gospels. Some of the writers noted that the hullabaloo was so great that the Jewish leaders begged Jesus to get the crowd to simmer down. Instead, He capitalized on this moment of public opportunity and returned to the temple precinct, where He cleansed the courts of commercial activity for the second time. The priests who profited from these commercial activities were livid but could do nothing because the crowds favored Jesus. It must be assumed that the Romans took no exception to what Jesus did in the temple that day. Roman soldiers were always on guard at festival seasons and would have been standing watch at the Antonia Fortress next to the temple courts. They would have observed what Jesus did, and if the proceedings had threatened Roman interests, they would have intervened. At the end of this first Palm Sunday, Jesus retreated up and over the Mount of Olives to Bethany, where He had friends and overnight protection.

For the next three days, Jesus came daily along the fifteen-furlong path from Bethany to Jerusalem to mix with the crowds in Jerusalem for Passover (there are eight furlongs in each mile). Contrary to His usual pattern, He apparently did no healings during these last few days of His mortal life, except for the healing done at the time of His capture in the Garden of Gethsemane, when He healed the servant wounded by Peter.

THE FIG TREE

The only miracle recorded during Passion Week is the withering of the fig tree, which seems counterintuitive: Why would Jesus punish a tree? The story is, however, symbolic. Jesus saw a tree that in midspring was fully leafed. Since the fig buds come out early in the spring, with the fruit maturing by May, it was reasonable for Jesus to believe that a fig tree with a full complement of leaves would offer fruit with which He could satisfy His hunger. Upon closer inspection, He found that the tree was all show and no harvest. Nearby stood the recently renovated temple, splendidly situated upon the fifty-acre platform Herod had made out of Mount Moriah.

These buildings gleamed with the promise of hosting a people dedicated to the covenant work commanded by God. But inside, Jesus found only avarice and oppression of the poor. Again, all show and no harvest. Jesus, with His insight into hearts and minds, observed: "And he said unto them in his doctrine, Beware of the scribes, which love to go in long clothing, and love salutations in the marketplaces, and the chief seats in the synagogues, and the uppermost rooms at feasts: which devour widows' houses, and for a pretence make long prayers: these shall receive greater damnation. And Jesus sat over against the treasury, and beheld how the people cast money into the treasury: and many that were rich cast in much. And there came a certain poor widow, and she threw in two mites, which make a farthing. And he called unto him his disciples, and saith unto them, Verily I say unto you, that this poor widow hath cast more in, than all they which have cast into the treasury: for all they did cast in of their abundance; but she of her want did cast in all that she had, even all her living" (Mark 12:38–44).

CONFRONTATIONS

No wonder Jesus focused His comments upon the scribes, Pharisees, and leading Jews of Jerusalem. They were afraid to openly arrest Him or treat Him with violence for He was the object of public goodwill. But they dreamed up mental exercises for Him and threw controversial questions at Him, not out of interest or curiosity but in an effort to confuse and discredit Him. Jesus was more than their match. He parried their question about His authority for taking action at the temple by asking them their opinions about the authority of John the Baptist. They didn't know how to answer without giving away the insincerity of their rhetoric, so He refused to answer their question.

In an effort to get Him to say something in opposition to Rome, they asked Him about whether tribute to a foreign power was appropriate. His answer has become an adage of the ages: Render unto Caesar that which is Caesar's and unto God that which is His (see Matthew 22:21). The Sadducees, with their peculiar and unscriptural doctrine of no resurrection, tried to snare Him with a discussion about marriage in the next life, and He would have none of it, pointing out that the God of Abraham, Isaac, and Jacob was a God of the living, a less-than-subtle reference to the fact that the patriarchs must themselves still be living despite the known fact that their tombs were located in Hebron. And finally, in lawyerly fashion, a questioner attempted to catch Him in a complicated and inherently conflictual discussion about the greatest of the commandments, to which He replied with a beautiful and simple teaching about God's expectations of man: "And one of the scribes came, and having heard them reasoning together, and perceiving that he had answered them well, asked him, Which is the first commandment of all? And Jesus answered him, The first of all the commandments is, Hear, O Israel; the Lord our God is one Lord: and thou shalt love the Lord thy God with all thy heart, and with all thy soul, and with all thy mind, and with all thy strength: this is the first commandment. And the second is like, namely this, thou shalt love thy neighbour as thyself. There is none other commandment greater than these. And the scribe said unto him, Well, Master, thou hast said the truth: for there is one God; and there is none other but he: and to love him with all the heart, and with all the understanding, and with all the soul, and with all the strength, and to love his neighbour as himself, is more than all whole burnt offerings and sacrifices. And when Jesus saw that he answered discreetly, he said unto him, thou art not far from the kingdom of God. And no man after that durst ask him any question" (Mark 12:28–34).

This is a poignant moment. Jesus is constantly under fire from those determined to find a credible way to bring a capital case against Him before the Roman authorities. As a group, they throw everything they have against Him, blind to His sheer intelligence and goodness. He is a healer, and they know it. He has raised people from the dead, and they know it. He has accused them of using the sacred temple precincts for commerce in search of personal profit and at the expense of the poor, and they know He is justified. And then one of them asks a doctrinal question requiring Jesus to think on His feet and summarize all commandments with the one statement of God's command that is most important, and Jesus just simply teaches His gospel to this scribe. I imagine Jesus making eye contact with this scribe and teaching him how to love God (by having faith) and his fellow men (by having charity). In doing so, Jesus made a friend and follower out of this former enemy. Aside from His atoning sacrifice, teaching the gospel was the most powerful thing Jesus did. His ability to intimately connect with others on a personal level and teach with such insight and love allowed Him to transform hearts and minds.

THE LAST SUPPER

On Thursday morning of the week of His passion, Jesus instructed Peter and John on how they should prepare the Passover meal. As He assembled in the upper room with His twelve closest associates, He told them how deeply He desired to eat this Passover meal with them.

Faith, which is love of God, is the first principle of the gospel and is founded upon the preeminent love God first had for us. But the second commandment, to love God's children, is the practical expression of faith: we cannot

A church located on Mount Zion near where tourists are shown the "upper room"

expect to have a meaningful relationship with God if we through fear let our love of men wax cold. Jesus taught this supreme principle of love at His final Passover: "He that hath my commandments, and keepeth them, he it is that loveth me" (John 14:21). "If a man love me, he will keep my words" (John 14:21). "If ye keep my commandments, ye shall abide in my love" (John 15:10).

At that same Passover meal and while walking to the Garden of Gethsemane to begin the ultimate act of love, Jesus stated, "A new commandment I give unto you, that ye love one another; as I have loved you, that ye also love one another. By this shall all men know that ye are my disciples, if ye have love one to another" (John 13:34). And then He restated it: "This is my commandment, that ye love one another, as I have loved you. Greater love hath no man than this, that a man lay down his life for his friends" (John 15:12–13). But He wasn't finished and restated it again: "These things I command you, that ye love one another" (John 15:17).

Jesus begins this final teaching by washing their feet, saying: "If I then, your Lord and Master, have washed your feet; ye also ought to wash one another's feet. For I have given you an example, that ye should do as I have done to you" (John 13:14–15). And Jesus ended this teaching by praying for His friends, saying, "I have declared unto them thy name, and will declare it: that the love wherewith thou has loved me may be in them, and I in them" (John 17:26). As we overcome our fears and serve each other, we serve God and become the answer to Christ's prayer.

GETHSEMANE

From the upper room where the last supper was held, Jesus led His Apostles in the dark across the brook Kidron to the Garden of Gethsemane, which means "olive press."

There, the scriptures record, "And they came to a place which was named Gethsemane: and he saith to his disciples, Sit ye here, while I shall pray. And he taketh with him Peter and James and John, and began to be sore amazed, and to be very heavy; and saith unto them, My soul is exceeding

The Garden of Gethsemane

The Garden of Gethsemane

sorrowful unto death: tarry ye here, and watch. And he went forward a little, and fell on the ground, and prayed that, if it were possible, the hour might pass from him. And he said, Abba, Father, all things are possible unto thee; take away this cup from me: nevertheless not what I will, but what thou wilt" (Mark 14:32–36).

Even Jesus was amazed at the immensity of the price of the Atonement. Luke, in his Gospel, says that blood poured from the Savior like sweat. But the cup could not pass from Jesus because if He could withstand all evil, He could help the rest of us resist the smaller portions of evil we all face. Jesus later told Joseph Smith what this sacrifice cost: "For behold, I, God, have suffered these things for all, that they might not suffer if they would repent; but if they would not repent they must suffer even as I; which suffering caused myself, even God, the greatest of all, to tremble because of pain, and to bleed at every pore, and to suffer both body and spirit—and would that I might not drink the bitter cup, and shrink—nevertheless, glory be to the Father, and I partook and finished my preparations unto the children of men" (D&C 19:16–19).

ILLEGAL TRIALS

Meanwhile, Judas, having realized that Jesus would be staying this night in Jerusalem, went to inform the priests. This was the real treachery of Judas: providing the intelligence that Jesus would not be overnight in Bethany, where He had friends and safety. Judas probably took the priests first to the upper room and then, finding Jesus gone, to Gethsemane, where Jesus often spent time. After His capture, Jesus was taken first to Annas, the previous high priest and father-in-law of Caiaphas, the current high priest. This was an illegal inquiry, as was the next, which occurred in the home of Caiaphas.

The priests attempted to come up with a case for a capital crime against Jesus. He was interrogated, which was also illegal. Jewish law required that legal cases were to be brought without requiring the accused to testify against himself; furthermore, the matter should be conducted in public,

Steps, said to be of first-century-AD origin, leading from the Kidron Valley to the home of Caiaphas, the high priest who held Jesus captive the night before the Crucifixion

during business hours, in the court building. When Jesus protested, He was slapped across the face. They brought witnesses who could not agree with each other. They tried Him on the eve of a Sabbath and a holy day, which was also illegal. They bullied Him into making a statement. The record is clear that the Sanhedrin had predetermined the verdict and wanted an excuse to exact capital punishment. After they convicted Jesus, they left Him until morning when the Roman authorities would be available. They filled the time by blindfolding Him, hitting Him, and taunting Him to prophesy who had hit Him.

The priests refused to go into the Roman hall of justice lest they make themselves unclean, undoubtedly the most hypocritical act recorded in scripture. Traditional Christian history places this event at the Antonia Fortress, and the Via Dolorosa in the Old City of Jerusalem begins where this fortress is thought to have been located. (*Via Dolorosa*, which means "way or path of pain or distress," is the name given to the pathway traditionally thought as the path Jesus traversed from His trial before Pilate to the place where He was crucified. The Antonia Fortress was a military building on the north side of the temple complex and was built explicitly so that Roman soldiers could look into the temple courts and observe what was happening. For instance, when the Apostle Paul was thought by Jews to have violated the sanctity of the temple and a riot ensued, threatening his life, a contingent of soldiers from the Antonia Fortress quickly ran into the temple precincts and rescued him.)

PILATE

However, it is much more likely that Pontius Pilate would not have stayed at the Antonia Fortress, which was in essence a military barracks. Rather, he would have overnighted in Herod's Palace, located on the western edge of the city, near where David's Citadel is now found.

The leaders of the Jews knew the Romans would not execute Jesus for blasphemy, so they falsely accused Him of rebellion against Caesar. Pilate took Jesus into the hall of justice alone and asked: "Art thou the King of the Jews? Jesus answered him, Sayest thou this thing of thyself, or did others tell it thee of me? Pilate answered, Am I a Jew? Thine own nation and the chief priests have delivered thee unto me: What hast thou done? Jesus answered, My kingdom is not of this world: if my kingdom were of this world, then would my servants fight, that I should not be delivered to the Jews: but now is my kingdom not from hence" (John 18:33–38). Jesus asked Pilate the meaning of his question about Christ being king. When Pilate made it clear he was only concerned about whether Jesus considered Himself to be a king of this world, Jesus explained that His was a spiritual leadership. Upon this testimony was Jesus acquitted.

The Citadel of David, part of the five-hundred-year-old Ottoman Empire wall around the Old City of Jerusalem

The ruins of King Herod's palace in Jerusalem

The Sanhedrin was furious about the verdict. Pilate decided to send Jesus to Herod Antipas, puppet king of Galilee, who was in Jerusalem for Passover. Herod Antipas was also likely staying in his father's Jerusalem palace. Herod had killed John the Baptist, and therefore Jesus refused to speak to Herod, who finally sent Him back to Pilate.

Pilate found himself in a quandary with this trial. His solution was to propose a compromise—he wanted to appease the Jews by convicting Jesus of treason but then release Him as the traditional prisoner of leniency because Pilate knew Jesus was innocent. But the leaders of the Jews were not dissuaded from their purpose and began calling for Jesus to die. The same crowd that had hailed Jesus just four days before as a son of David now called for Him to die, undoubtedly having been agitated by the Jewish leaders trying to foment a reversal of public opinion. At this point, Pilate's wife

The rock face in East Jerusalem near the Garden Tomb thought to be Golgotha

wrote to her husband this note: "Have nothing to do with that just man: for I have suffered many things this day in a dream because of Him" (Matthew 27:19). At this point, Pilate washed his hands of the matter.

The first stage of crucifixion was scourging—a brutal whipping intended to weaken the victim and shorten the time of death. During Jesus's scourging, a Roman soldier taunted Him with a crown of thorns. Pilate stepped in to stop the barbarism and for a third time tried to get Jesus off by saying, "I find no fault in Him." The Jews replied, "We have a law and by our law he ought to die, because he made himself the Son of God" (John 19:7). Pilate took Jesus back into the hall of justice alone and questioned Him.

However, at about nine or ten o'clock that morning, Jesus was led away to Golgotha to be crucified.

GOLGOTHA

Traditional Christianity places Golgotha within what is now the Church of the Holy Sepulchre, and therefore the Via Dolorosa progresses from where the Antonia Fortress is thought to have been to the Church of the Holy Sepulchre, which is often deemed the holiest spot in Christendom. Today, seven Christian denominations jointly own this church, and its sprawling interior is consequently disjointed, noisy, and often jammed with competing believers.

It is my opinion that Golgotha was not located within what is now the Church of the Holy Sepulchre. The site of a crucifixion during the second temple period would have been very definitely outside the city walls and next to a major road, a Roman practice of providing a visual deterrent against criminal behavior. It is possible the location now occupied by the Church of the Holy Sepulchre would have been outside the city walls at the time Pontius Pilate washed his hands of the execution of Jesus of

Entrance to the Church of the Holy Sepulchre

The aedicula over the tomb of Jesus underneath the dome of the Church of the Holy Sepulchre

Nazareth, but it is not as likely that this site was next to a major road or highway.

There is a site, however, that fits these criteria and also has a rock outcropping that bears some resemblance to a skull. Today, it is located next to a bus station in East Jerusalem and immediately to the north of the Garden Tomb. Further, this site would likely have served as a place of execution by stoning, since stoning usually commenced with the victim being pushed off a cliff before being finished off with hand-thrown stones.

Therefore, in my opinion, at about midmorning on the first Good Friday, Jesus was led from King Herod's Jerusalem palace, near what is now the Jaffa Gate of the Old City, to Golgotha, which was outside the city walls and along the road to Damascus, later made famous by the journey of Saul when the resurrected Jesus confronted and converted him, transforming him into the Apostle Paul.

At noon on that first Good Friday, the light of the sun was obscured.

At three in the afternoon, Jesus called with a loud voice, "My God, my God, why hast thou forsaken me?" (Mark 15:34), signaling a return of his solitary suffering in the garden. When that moment of intense suffering passed, Jesus knew His task was complete, and He chose to die, saying, "Father into thy hands I commend my spirit" (Luke 23:46). Immediately, an earthquake shook the ground, and the veil of the temple was rent. John the Beloved testified that Jesus did in fact die on the cross: "But one of the soldiers with a spear pierced his side, and forthwith came there out blood and water. And he that saw it bare record, and his record is true: and he knoweth that he saith true, that ye might believe" (John 19:34–5).

Jesus died both a temporal and a spiritual death during His day of suffering. He alone among all mortals was the Only Begotten of God the Father and therefore was born with immortality. It follows that He alone could choose to give up His life, which He did, as a gift to all of us. He alone among mortals never acted wrongly such that He separated Himself spiritually from our Father in Heaven. God chose to leave Jesus alone in the garden and on the cross so that "he descended below all things, in that he comprehended all things, that he might be in all and through all things, the light of truth" (D&C 88:6).

In dying, Jesus proved that the authority and power of this world is weak compared to the mightier power of people who love and think of others before themselves. All of us have chosen to remove ourselves from God through sin. In doing so, we've caused ourselves and others to suffer. Because Jesus experienced the withdrawal of His Father's presence, He knows unequivocally what we are going through. Said Alma, "And he shall go forth, suffering pains and afflictions and temptations of every kind; and this that the word might be fulfilled which saith he will take upon him the pains and the sicknesses of his people. And he will take upon him death, that he may loose the bands of death which bind his people; and he will take upon him their infirmities, that his bowels may be filled with mercy, according to the flesh, that he may know according to the flesh how to succor his people according to their infirmities. Now the Spirit knoweth all things; nevertheless the Son of God suffereth according to the flesh that he might take upon him the sins of his people, that he might blot out their transgressions according to the power of his deliverance" (Alma 7:11–13).

DAMASCUS

Biblical minimalists don't accept the scriptural account of the Atonement accomplished by Jesus Christ, and that is their loss, for they miss out on the "hope of the promise" offered by Christ to all mankind of which Paul testified before Festus and Agrippa. Essentially, biblical minimalists stand against the message of Christ just as Paul did before his conversion. As he himself says, "I verily thought with myself, that I ought to do many things contrary to the name of Jesus of Nazareth . . . and many of the saints did I shut up in prison . . . and when they were put to death, I gave my voice against them . . . and being exceedingly mad against them, I persecuted them even unto strange cities" (Acts 26:9–11).

Paul goes on to relate his astonishing experience on the road to Damascus—how at midday he saw a light brighter than the sun and heard a voice speaking Hebrew, a voice that identified its owner as "Jesus whom thou persecutest" (Acts 26:15). On the spot, Paul is called to the ministry and sent to the Gentiles "to open their eyes, and to turn them from darkness to light, and from the power of Satan unto God, that they may receive forgiveness of sins, and inheritance among them which are sanctified by faith" (Acts 26:18).

Paul then centers in on King Agrippa, a man known to have studied the Hebrew scriptures and therefore likely to be prepared to hear fairly Paul's pronouncement of the hope promised in the Old Testament: "Having therefore obtained help of God, I continue unto this day, witnessing both to small and great, saying none other things than those which the prophets and Moses did say should come: that Christ should suffer, and that he should be the first that should rise form the dead, and should shew light unto the people, and to the Gentiles. . . . For the king knoweth of these things, before whom also I speak freely: for I am persuaded that none of these things are hidden from him; for this thing was not done in a corner" (Acts 26:22–26).

King Agrippa seems to have been touched by Paul's words and almost accepts Paul's witness. Sadly, today's biblical minimalists, who themselves have a background in scripture, seem untouched by the witness of the sacrifice of the Savior, to which all scripture, covenants, and ordinances point.

Like Agrippa and the minimalists, we too have a choice. If we decide to believe and allow the hope of the promise to take root in our hearts, we can become, as Paul did, a new creature in Christ. When that marvelous transformation takes place, we see with new eyes, understanding with increased clarity our true relationship with God and our true value in His eyes. We become filled with charity toward all people and steadfast and immovable in our devotion and service to God. That doesn't mean we won't have trials and suffering. Like Paul, we will still have storms and shipwrecks in our daily lives. We will be persecuted for our faith. But we will find that when we enter into the covenant, we are filled with God's love, and that brings tremendous peace into our lives and power to act in His name to bless those around us.

THE RESURRECTION

For those who believe, the tenderness of the Resurrection story, particularly as it is told from Mary Magdalene's perspective, offers both sweet confirmation as well as strong arguments for the veracity of these events: "The first day of the week cometh Mary Magdalene early, when it was yet dark, unto the sepulchre, and seeth the stone taken away from the sepulchre. Then she runneth, and cometh to Simon Peter, and to the other disciple, whom Jesus loved, and saith unto them, They have taken away the Lord out of the sepulchre, and we know not where they have laid him. Peter therefore went forth, and that other disciple, and came to the sepulchre. . . . For as yet they knew not the scripture, that he must rise again from the dead. Then the disciples went away again unto their own home. But Mary stood without at the sepulchre weeping: and as she wept, she stooped down, and looked into the sepulchre, and seeth two angels in white sitting, the one at the head, and the other at the feet, where the body of Jesus had lain. And they say unto her, Woman, why weepest thou? She saith unto them, Because they have taken away my Lord, and I know not where they have laid him. And when she had thus said, she turned herself back, and saw Jesus standing, and knew not that it was Jesus. Jesus saith unto her, Woman, why weepest thou? whom seekest thou? She, supposing him to be the gardener, saith unto him, Sir, if thou have borne him hence, tell me where thou hast laid him, and I will take him away. Jesus saith unto her, Mary. She turned herself, and saith unto him, Rabboni; which is to say, Master. Jesus saith unto

A close-up of the Garden Tomb

her, Touch me not; for I am not yet ascended to my Father: but go to my brethren, and say unto them, I ascend unto my Father, and your Father; and to my God, and your God" (John 20:1–3, 9–17).

John, who wrote this account, remembers that he and others had not yet grasped what Jesus had taught repeatedly—that He would die at the hand of the Jewish leadership and then rise again. Even though Jesus had raised people from the dead, demonstrating His power over life and death, the disciples didn't fully understand what that meant, neither for themselves nor for all of humanity.

To tell the story of the Resurrection, John chooses to feature the experience of Mary Magdalene. This is an unusual perspective for a man of the first century AD because women were not considered official witnesses in the Jewish courts. If John were inventing the Resurrection story, it is unlikely he would have Mary Magdalene featured so prominently as the first witness. But, as has already been noted, there are those who believe her presence in the Resurrection story as the first person to witness it makes it likely that she was married to Jesus and therefore that this is actually what happened. Certainly, her behavior on this occasion—rising before dawn, weeping when she believes the body stolen, and running to Jesus's closest friends for help—conforms to expectations for the behavior of a spouse. But the very tender meeting between the two in which she recognizes His voice and instinctively holds Him underscores how close and tender her relationship

Looking out from within the Garden Tomb

must have been with Jesus. The Joseph Smith Translation of this passage changes the words "Touch me not" to "Hold me not," and His explanation for needing to leave her so soon after meeting her that He must report to His Father in Heaven is perhaps the only cause for separation that she, were she His wife, could have accepted under the circumstances.

For those Christians today who do not accept that Jesus was either crucified or interred on the site now occupied by the Church of the Holy Sepulchre, the spot known as the Garden Tomb, located near a possible site for Golgotha, provides a popular alternative. The Garden

The Garden Tomb showing the groove in which the stone door would have fit

Tomb is an inviting place presently located within a garden, which fits with John 19:41. But some archeologists date it back to the eighth and seventh centuries BC, contradicting Matthews's description of a newly hewn tomb. It is probable that an as-yet-undiscovered cave in this neighborhood was actually the site of the Resurrection. But the actual location matters far less than the fact that the resurrected Lord appeared in the flesh, proving He had broken the gates of hell and conquered death and that because He did so, each of us will one day be resurrected.

Beginning with Mary Magdalene, the circle of people who were personal witnesses to the Resurrection grew rapidly that first Easter Sunday and on through the following seven weeks until Jesus ascended to heaven just before Pentecost. John and the other three Gospel authors carefully built their case that the Resurrection was a reality. They recited the facts:

Jesus really did die on the cross. His body was interred and guarded. It was widely known that He had prophesied that He would rise, and so the Jewish leadership took pains to be sure that Jesus's friends did not steal the body and pretend He had risen. The leaders never could produce the body of Jesus even though they asserted it must still exist.

Meanwhile, dozens of people testified that they had seen Him, that they had handled His scarred hands and side, that He had spoken to them, and that He had eaten with them. This was not a story that evolved with time as an oral tradition with repeated telling over decades or generations. What emerged immediately after that first Easter Sunday was a dedicated cadre of witnesses willing to risk everything, including life and freedom, to tell the story. Even some opponents became convinced. One of those, Saul, later known as Paul, became the author of the earliest written records now available about this most transcendent event in human history, the fulfillment of the hope of the promise, which he later described to Herod Agrippa.

CHAPTER 6

JERUSALEM AFTER JESUS: HOW THE JEWS HAVE GATHERED

As Jesus had prophesied, Jerusalem was destroyed by a pagan army for the second time in 70 AD. This war began in 66 AD as a revolt of Jewish religious zealots against Roman rule and targeted Roman citizens in Jerusalem. The Roman governor responded by plundering the temple and arresting senior Jewish citizens. Jewish insurgents in turn overran the Roman military garrison in Judea, inducing the Roman legion in Syria to attack. The Roman legion, however, was ambushed en route to Jerusalem, and six thousand Roman soldiers were killed. Nero, the emperor, assigned Vespasian the task of crushing the rebellion, with Vespasian's son Titus as second in command.

Vespasian invaded Judea with four legions in 67 AD and began the methodical destruction of all things Jewish, finally placing the capital city under siege in 70 AD just before the Passover Feast. When Vespasian was

The remains of a Roman legion camp outlined in the Judean Desert below Masada

The ramp built by the Roman army to breach the fortifications at Masada

called back to Rome to assume leadership of the empire after Nero's death, Titus finished the conquest of Jerusalem.

In the end, Jesus was correct: not one stone of the second temple was left upon another once the Romans finished destroying Jerusalem. The Romans were so methodical in their destruction that they followed up their ruination of Jerusalem by searching out those few Jews in hiding around the Dead Sea and finished them off. Both Qumran, the home of the Jewish sect known as the Essenes and the place where the Dead Sea Scrolls were found, and Masada, King Herod's mountain hideaway, were attacked and finished off by the Roman legions, though neither of these places had any real strategic importance. The Romans were simply making a statement: Don't mess with us.

Sadly, the Jews forgot that lesson over the next sixty years. Perhaps they hoped the prophecy about rebuilding the first temple seventy years after its destruction would apply to the second temple as well. Or maybe it was that the Romans gradually became increasingly heavy-handed in their attempts to Hellenize every people and province within their jurisdiction. For instance, they outlawed circumcision among the Jews, thus enraging Jewish religious sentiment. More likely, the Jews who had been banned from Jerusalem after the Roman victory in 70 AD became concerned about the plans for the city, which Hadrian, the Roman emperor early in the second century, had articulated upon his visit in 132 AD. Jerusalem was to be renamed Aelia Capitolina, after

Judean Desert mountains next to Qumran

Ruins atop Masada, including a pile of stone projectiles hurled at Masada by the Roman army during the siege of Masada

One of the many caves at Qumran where scrolls were found

both Hadrian and the Roman deity Jupiter, and restyled as a Roman colony with a temple to Jupiter on Temple Mount

The Jewish community in Jerusalem would have understood the use of Temple Mount as a space for a pagan temple to be "an abomination that maketh desolate" (Daniel 11:31), which had previously occurred during the second-temple era when the Seleucid king Antiochus had pursued an aggressive Hellenization policy in Judea that included forcing Jews to worship Greek gods and placing a statue of Zeus on the altar of the temple. During that time, from 167 to 166 BC, the Maccabees led a successful revolt against this Seleucid oppression, culminating in the cleansing and rededication of the temple, which is still celebrated among Jews at Hannukah. That the memories of this terrible desecration of the temple still haunted the Jews can be seen in the reference Jesus made in His prophecy about the destruction of Jerusalem; He said the destruction would be imminent "when ye therefore shall see the abomination of desolation, spoken of by Daniel the prophet, stand in the holy place" (Matthew 24:15).

These plans, plus the ongoing economic trend initiated by King Herod

Ruins at Qumran, including a mikveh, or cleansing bath

(and multiplied by uncaring Roman administrators after Herod's death) to rob Jews of their subsistence farms and turn them into starving share-croppers, gave Jewish communities no real stake in the Roman program and therefore nothing to lose. In addition, there was always an underlying messianic expectation among Jewish believers who hoped God would step in and solve their national woes. All together, these factors kindled a massive uprising in 132 AD, much bigger than the first Jewish revolt in 70 AD.

SECOND REVOLT

This revolt was led by Simon bar Kokhba (Simon the son of a star), a reference to a messianic prophecy stating: "I shall see him, but not now: I shall behold him, but not nigh: there shall come a Star out of Jacob" (Numbers 24:17). A contemporaneous Jewish sage, Rabbi Akiva, thinking that Simon really was the messiah, gave him the name with reference to the prophecy in Numbers. That messianic assumption was based upon the initial success Simon bar Kokhba enjoyed as the leader of the revolt. His military victories allowed him to rule as prince of Israel independent from Rome for more than two years. He mustered a large army of up to four hundred thousand Jewish warriors, partially by punishing Jews who did not want to fight. Many of the nonfighters were Christian Jews who would not accept Simon as the messiah since they were no longer looking for such a leader to appear. As it turned out, driving Christians out of Judea by punishing them for nonparticipation in the revolt was a blessing to the developing Christian church because being driven away from the revolution ultimately saved the lives of many Christian Jews.

As was true in 70 AD when Roman legions found it difficult to defeat the Jewish army, during the bar Kokhba rebellion, they simply called in more legions. As many as ten legions participated in putting down the rebellion, far more soldiers than were at the disposal of Titus when he burned the second temple. The Roman army did its usual thorough, methodical job of finishing off the Jews. In this case, the final siege was not in Jerusalem itself—which bar Kokhba had initially occupied but soon found too ruined to be defendable—but in the Judean hills at Betar, the ruins of which are now near a Palestinian town called Khirbet-al-Yahud, or "ruin of the Jews."

As many as six hundred thousand Jews lost their lives in the rebellion and uncountable more in the hunger and chaos caused by the war. After the revolt was vanquished, the Romans built Aeolia Capitolina to their taste anyway, the Jews were banished not just from Jerusalem but from all Judea, and the name of that Roman province was changed by Emperor Hadrian to Syria Palestina, ostensibly after the ancient enemy of Israel, the Philistines. This defeat was essentially the end of Jewish influence in what was Judea for more than 1500 years. During a recent visit I made to Israel, a Jewish guide, while telling the story of Hadrian in Jerusalem added, "May his name not be remembered" each time he mentioned the emperor. Somehow, Hadrian is still held responsible for nearly two thousand years of Jewish diaspora and distress.

The Kokhba revolt was a bitter end to Jewish interests in Jerusalem.

Zodiac mosaics on the floor of a Byzantine-era synagogue

Jews were allowed to visit Jerusalem one day each year and then only to pray and mourn over the lost temple at the Wailing Wall, which is how the western retaining wall of Temple Mount built originally by King Herod got that name. Christians came to believe that Simon bar Kokhba was the false messiah Jesus had prophesied of before His Crucifixion: "Then if any man shall say unto you, Lo, here is Christ, or there; believe it not. For there shall arise false Christs, and false prophets, and shall shew great signs and wonders; insomuch that, if it were possible, they shall deceive the very elect" (Matthew 24:23–24). Rabbi Akiva, who called Simon bar Kokhba the son of the star, surely qualified as one of the very elect among Jews who was fooled by the false messiah.

Jewish religious thought and practice was forever changed by the disastrous outcome of the bar Kokhba rebellion. Forced to do without temple festivals and rites, and without any real hope of ever seeing a messiah, Jewish worship became increasingly centered on the Torah, led by the only surviving sect of pre-Christian Jewry—the Pharisees. The Messiah became a metaphorical idea, or mystical presence. Most Jews left or were carried

Schematic of zodiac mosaics found on the floor of a Byzantine-era synagogue

Close-up of zodiac mosaics from the floor of a Byzantine-era synagogue

away from Judea, now called Syria Palestina. The Diaspora became home for Judaism, which managed the seemingly impossible task of keeping the faith separate and alive for millennia in hostile territory. For those Jews who managed to stay behind in Syria Palestina, it was often easier to stop insisting on purity in Judaic practice and simply join the Hellenistic movement the Romans inspired. That explains, I think, how the signs of the zodiac came to be the theme of more than one floor mosaic in second to fourth-century synagogues that have been unearthed in modern-day Israel.

THE BYZANTINE PERIOD AND MUSLIM RULE

Pagan Roman rule in Jerusalem, or Aelia Capitolina as it was then known, was followed by Byzantine rule beginning around the fourth century. The Byzantines were Romans who, after the conversion of Emperor Constantine, became Christians. They were not ruled from Rome anymore, but rather from Constantinople, which Constantine made the seat of the empire in 330 AD. Constantine had the challenge of reeducating Roman pagans to become Christian Byzantines, and he had expert help in this task. His mother, Queen Helena, came to Palestine at age seventy-nine and began searching out all of the important sites for Christian indoctrination. She knew she would be followed by countless numbers of pilgrims who would need places to see and stay while they were instructed about the origins of Christianity. So she identified places that fit both the religious and travel requirements, built churches and monuments, and generally provided for religious tourists to have a proper program while on their pilgrim's tour. Helena remains a force to be reckoned with for Christian pilgrims to this day.

As the Roman Empire waned and succumbed to invading pagan hordes from the north, the eastern edge of the empire came under attack by a new monotheistic force: Islam. Beginning in the seventh century AD, Muslims would rule Jerusalem until the twentieth century, except for a small sliver of time during the Crusades.

Unlike the capture of Jerusalem by both the Babylonian and Roman forces, the takeover by Muslim armies in 638 AD was peaceful. The leader of the Muslim forces, Caliph Omar, visited Jerusalem and, with advice from Jewish counselors, cleared Temple Mount of the decay and debris the Byzantines had allowed to accumulate (a witness of Jesus's prophecy) and established there a place of Muslim worship. A few Jews were even allowed to resettle in Jerusalem and worship in the vicinity of Temple Mount. Eventually, Muslim leadership was consolidated by the establishment of the Umayyad dynasty, which held power until 750 AD with governance by both Damascus and Jerusalem. The Dome of the Rock was completed in 691 AD, followed soon thereafter by the Al-Aqsa Mosque,

The Horns of Hattin, where Saladin's Islamic army defeated the Christian Crusaders

both of which can be seen today on Temple Mount. But even with these major construction projects, Jerusalem was increasingly relegated to provincial-town status.

After the end of the Umayyad dynasty, the Abbasid dynasty transferred the capital of the Islamic empire from Damascus farther east and away from Jerusalem to Baghdad. The Abbasid dynasty in turn gave way to the Fatimid dynasty, which captured Palestine in 969 AD. The Fatimids were briefly replaced by Seljuk Turks who brought Sunni Muslim leadership back to Jerusalem when they burned the city in 1071. In turn, they lost control of Jerusalem again in 1098 to the Fatimids, who were Shiites who ruled briefly again until the Crusader Knights sacked Jerusalem in 1099, ruling there until 1187.

Saladin, the leader of the Muslim army that prevailed against the Crusaders at the Horns of Hattin, reestablished Jerusalem as a Muslim holy city and allowed Jews to return and settle in the southeast corner, creating the Jewish Quarter near the Western Wall, exactly where it still is today. Saladin was the first leader of the Ayyubid dynasty, which ruled in Jerusalem until 1244 AD. Though Saladin and his successor, Ayyubids, took the title "Protector of Jerusalem" in general, like most of the Muslim rulers, they did little to keep decay from within the Holy City. (It's tragically ironic that neither the Muslims nor the Byzantine (or for that matter, Crusader) Christians cared much about Jerusalem except to deny it to the Jews, who really cared about it.)

At the close of the Ayyubid era, control of Egypt, Syria, and Palestine, including Jerusalem, was taken by the Mamelukes, who retained power for nearly three hundred years. With virtually no defenses, Jerusalem had fallen into disrepair, and the Mamelukes were Muslims without any apparent interest in the third holiest place in Islam. The Mameluke seat of power was Cairo, and Jerusalem was considered a lower-echelon provincial town. Jews and Christians were not treated well by the Mamelukes, and many left the Holy City, with the population falling from forty thousand at the end of the Crusader era to about ten thousand at the time the Mamelukes lost control of Jerusalem to the Ottomans in 1517 AD.

The second sultan of the Ottomans, Sulieman the Magnificent, actually cared about Jerusalem enough to make substantial efforts to upgrade and rebuild the city. He is responsible for the wall around the Old City, which still stands today. He also improved the municipal water system and refurbished the Dome of the Rock. Sulieman also made a formal denouncement of blood libels against the Jews on the advice of his favorite Jewish physician, Moses Hamon. For the first time in centuries, there seemed to be a hope that Jerusalem could once again become a beautiful city.

That hope, however, was short-lived. Subsequent sultans relegated Jerusalem to backwater status and cared only about whether the population of the city was punitively taxed. Jerusalem and Palestine went into a decline that continued until into the nineteenth century. Poverty was the norm in Jerusalem, especially for Jews. The streets were unpaved. The few thousand inhabitants of the city lived in filth and stench. Much of the city consisted of abandoned and disintegrating houses and deserted fields. Crime was endemic. More than one thousand years of Muslim rule had brought Jerusalem to its lowest point, seemingly abandoned by God.

THREE PROPHETS BEAR WITNESS

But, as many Old Testament prophets observed, it was not God who abandoned Jerusalem but the people of Jerusalem, the house of Israel, who abandoned God. This theme is a dominant motif running through their prophecies and observations:

> The ox knoweth his owner, and the ass his master's crib: but Israel doth not know, my people doth not consider. Ah sinful nation, a people laden with iniquity, a seed of evildoers, children that are corrupters: they have forsaken the Lord, they have provoked the Holy One of Israel unto anger, they are gone away backward. (Isaiah 1:3–4)

Woe unto them that call evil good, and good evil; that put darkness for light, and light for darkness; that put bitter for sweet, and sweet for bitter! Woe unto them that are wise in their own eyes, and prudent in their own sight! Woe unto them that are mighty to drink wine, and men of strength to mingle strong drink: which justify the wicked for reward, and take away the righteousness of the righteous from him! Therefore as the fire devoureth the stubble, and the flame consumeth the chaff, so their root shall be as rottenness, and their blossom shall go up as dust: because they have cast away the law of the Lord of hosts, and despised the word of the Holy One of Israel. Therefore is the anger of the Lord kindled against his people, and he hath stretched forth his hand against them, and hath smitten them: and the hills did tremble, and their carcases were torn in the midst of the streets. For all this his anger is not turned away, but his hand is stretched out still. (Isaiah 5:20–25)

Israel was holiness unto the Lord, and the firstfruits of his increase: . . . And I brought you into a plentiful country, to eat the fruit thereof and the goodness thereof; but when ye entered, ye defiled my land, and made mine heritage an abomination. . . . For my people have committed two evils; they have forsaken me the fountain of living waters, and hewed them out cisterns, broken cisterns, that can hold no water. . . . Yet I had planted thee a noble vine, wholly a right seed: how then art thou turned into the degenerate plant of a strange vine unto me? . . . Wherefore will ye plead with me? Ye all have transgressed against me, saith the Lord. . . . Can a maid forget her ornaments, or a bride her attire? yet my people have forgotten me days without number. (Jeremiah 2:3–32)

Son of man, thou dwellest in the midst of a rebellious house, which have eyes to see, and see not; they have ears to hear, and hear not: for they are a rebellious house. (Ezekiel 12:2)

Isaiah, Jeremiah, and Ezekiel, the three major prophets of the house of Israel at the time of the destruction first of the Northern Kingdom (in Isaiah's lifetime) and then of the Southern Kingdom, or kingdom of Judah (in the lifetimes of Jeremiah and Ezekiel), had as their principal calling the burden of warning the people of Israel that God's protection and prosperity belonged only to those who embraced the principles of happiness embodied in God's commandments.

Jerusalem emerged as the capital of all twelve tribes as David built a city during a time when the regional powers of Mesopotamia and Egypt were relatively weak. During the reigns of David and Solomon, Jerusalem was a powerhouse, its temple built using the best materials from the entire region. But the people of Israel mistook their foremost position among nations at that time, believing that their national success was due to their industry, cleverness, and military capacity. They forgot how they'd come to inhabit the land of Canaan, by whose hand they prospered, and how best to maintain a peaceful, happy society. They did not notice the gradual loss of peace and prosperity inherent in going away backward, forgetting God days without number, and having eyes and ears but seeing and hearing not.

The people of the Northern Kingdom, defeated brutally by the Assyrians, were taken captive, scattered, and never returned. The people of the Southern Kingdom, the kingdom of Judah, including the city of Jerusalem, were defeated by the Babylonians and taken captive to Babylon, but seventy years later, some returned to rebuild Jerusalem and the temple. For a time, it must have seemed to the Jews of the second temple period that they had permanently succeeded where their ancestors had failed. King Herod, though not a Jew by birth, rebuilt and expanded the temple and its courts in a marvelous manner; the second temple was considered a wonder of the ancient world. King Herod was second only to the Roman Caesar in wealth and influence. But this apparent renaissance of Jewish beauty and accomplishment was an illusion, as Titus and his legions proved in 70 AD.

The series of Christian and Muslim rulers in Jerusalem in the nearly two thousand years after the burning of the second temple could have re-created a wondrous city and society there. The Islamic Golden Age began not long after the Dome of the Rock was built in Jerusalem and influenced cultural life in the Muslim world for several centuries. Scholars from all over the Muslim world of that era lived and practiced their various professions in Baghdad, then the largest city in the world. Advances in philosophy, medicine, and mathematics are among the achievements of the Islamic Golden Age. Paper-making became more generally available. Algebra was invented. Classics from ancient Greece were translated and preserved. The science of clinical trials for new medical treatments was first explored. Somehow, none of these bold pursuits of human curiosity and invention in Baghdad inspired any interest or action in Jerusalem, which over the years leading up to the blood and suffering of the Crusades seemed to simply drift into irrelevant obscurity.

After the Crusades, when Europe began its own intellectual reawakening, probably inspired in part by what the Crusaders had seen in the impressive achievements of Islamic culture, the Mediterranean rim, except for Jerusalem and Palestine, became home of the Renaissance. While Europeans were opening up to science and artistic achievement, and while the Enlightenment was driving new forms of governance and philosophy, Jerusalem continued to wither under the rule of Mamelukes and Ottomans. By the early part of the eighteenth century, there were fewer than ten thousand residents in Jerusalem. Likewise, Palestine in general was a neglected, backward Ottoman province with little to recommend it. The land was forsaken and ruined, as foreseen by the prophets Jeremiah and Micah: "Therefore thus saith the Lord of hosts; Because ye have not heard my words, behold, I will send and take all the families of the north . . . and will utterly destroy them, and make them an astonishment, and an hissing, and perpetual desolations. Moreover I will take from them the voice of mirth, and the voice of gladness, the voice of the bridegroom, and the voice of the bride, the sound of the millstones, and the light of the candle. And this whole land shall be a desolation, and an astonishment" (Jeremiah 25:8–11).

"Therefore shall Zion for your sake be plowed as a field, and Jerusalem shall become heaps" (Micah 3:12).

By the end of the nineteenth century, Palestine and Jerusalem, though still under Ottoman control, were slowly awakening from desolation into new life with tens of thousands of new inhabitants and new worldwide interest in events occurring in the "Holy Land." Jews had begun returning to their ancestral homeland and anticipating the day when a Jewish government would lead. That this transformation would someday take place had been a passionate subject among the Old Testament prophets who had witnessed the scattering of Israel by the Assyrians and Babylonians.

Isaiah

Isaiah was the prophet in Jerusalem during the reign of King Hezekiah. It was Isaiah who saw the hordes of warriors from Assyria at the gates of Jerusalem after they had destroyed the Northern Kingdom of Israel (which kingdom was associated with the tribe of Ephraim, among nine others) and prophesied that they would not succeed in taking the Holy City. But after King Hezekiah had unwisely shown the temple treasury to a delegation of Babylonians, Isaiah prophesied that Jerusalem would be defeated by their army. Burdened with the knowledge that the kingdom of Judah would be destroyed, Isaiah balanced the heartbreak of that reality with revelations of great hope and promise. He often spoke of a remarkable gathering of the Jews far off in the future.

In fact, beginning with Isaiah, the gathering of Israel became the dominant thread of prophetic pronouncement for the next several centuries. For members of The Church of Jesus Christ of Latter-day Saints familiar with the Book of Mormon, Isaiah's prophecies about the gathering have enjoyed particular emphasis given that many of them are repeated verbatim in 1 and 2 Nephi with additions and explanations by Jesus Himself while visiting with Lehi's descendants after His Resurrection.

Latter-day Saints have often heard (or voiced) complaints about the difficulties in comprehending the so-called Isaiah chapters in 1 and 2 Nephi. These chapters were written into the initial portions of the Book of Mormon by Nephi, who lived through the scattering of Israel and, as a result, was focused on how Israel would someday be gathered. His love for the writings of Isaiah, whose poetic prophecies about the gathering are a prime source of information and inspiration about it, is evident throughout his account.

Nephi's brother Jacob shared this fascination with the gathering and in his own portion of the sacred texts that became the Book of Mormon, he writes the parable of the wild and tame olive trees, an allegory about the gathering taken from the prophet Zenos, who is not found in the canon of the Old Testament. Jacob sums up what he knows about this gathering by saying: "How merciful is our God unto us, for he remembers the house of Israel, both roots and branches; and he stretches forth his hands unto them all the day long; and they are a stiff-necked and a gainsaying people; but as many as will not harden their hearts shall be saved in the kingdom of God. Wherefore, my beloved brethren, I beseech of you in words of soberness that ye would repent, and come with full purpose of heart, and cleave unto God as he cleaveth unto you. And while his arm of mercy is extended toward you in the light of the day, harden not your hearts" (Jacob 6:4–5).

Isaiah, Nephi, and Jacob are writing both for their contemporaries, who need reassurance that the scattering will not end God's interest in Israel, and for those who live in the day of gathering today. When Jesus visits the Americas after His Resurrection, He quotes Isaiah about the gathering of Israel, emphasizing the vital role of these prophecies: "A commandment I give unto you that ye search these things diligently; for great are the words of Isaiah" (3 Nephi 23:1). If we want to know what God intends to accomplish in our time and how we can cleave to God as He has cleaved to us, we need to pay attention to the prophets of the gathering, beginning with Isaiah, the first such prophet.

As I have read and reread the ancient gathering prophecies in the Old Testament, I have found the hardness of my modern heart melt away. Living through the scattering must have been an awful experience. Being forced from home by violence that killed thousands, then carried away captive to foreign cities, and there required to toil on public-works projects benefitting the captors—all of this would have been frightening and emotionally disabling. If I were suffering through that trial, I might doubt that God would ever care about me or my family again. But then, to have the prophecies of Isaiah read out loud, or those of Jeremiah, or, in Babylon, to listen to the prophet Ezekiel, was to hear the voice of heaven promising that Israel would be brought home again, that ancient promises would be fulfilled, and that I and my family might yet be acceptable to God.

Today, we who are living as the gathering is happening must also look for God's arm to be extended toward us in the light of day and harden not our hearts as we face our own challenges. We, too, must attend to the prophecies of the gathering. Below are selections from Isaiah detailing what he saw of the future gathering of Israel. Read these verses and then remind yourself of them as you read the summary that follows of how the modern State of Israel came into being.

> And he will lift up an ensign to the nations from far, and will hiss unto them from the end of the earth: and, behold, they shall come with speed swiftly: none shall be weary nor stumble among them; none shall slumber nor sleep; neither shall the girdle of their loins be loosed, nor the latchet of their shoes be broken. (Isaiah 5:26–27)

> And it shall come to pass in that day, that the Lord shall set his hand again the second time to recover the remnant of his people, which shall be left, from Assyria, and from Egypt, and from

Pathros, and from Cush, and from Elam, and from Shinar, and from Hamath, and from the islands of the sea. And he shall set up an ensign for the nations, and shall assemble the outcasts of Israel, and gather together the dispersed of Judah from the four corners of the earth. The envy also of Ephraim shall depart, and the adversaries of Judah shall be cut off: Ephraim shall not envy Judah, and Judah shall not vex Ephraim. (Isaiah 11:11–13)

For the Lord will have mercy on Jacob, and will yet choose Israel, and set them in their own land: and the strangers shall be joined with them, and they shall cleave to the house of Jacob. And the people shall take them, and bring them to their place: and the house of Israel shall possess them in the land of the Lord for servants and handmaids: and they shall take them captives, whose captives they were; and they shall rule over their oppressors. And it shall come to pass in the day that the Lord shall give thee rest from thy sorrow, and from thy fear, and from the hard bondage wherein thou wast made to serve. (Isaiah 14:1–3)

The wilderness and the solitary place shall be glad for them; and the desert shall rejoice, and blossom as the rose. It shall blossom abundantly, and rejoice even with joy and singing: and the ransomed of the Lord shall return, and come to Zion with songs and everlasting joy upon their heads: they shall obtain joy and gladness, and sorrow and sighing shall flee away. (Isaiah 35:1–2, 10)

Fear not: for I am with thee: I will bring thy seed from the east, and gather thee from the west; I will say to the north, Give up; and to the south, Keep not back: bring my sons from far, and my daughters from the ends of the earth; even every one that is called by my name: for I have created him for my glory, I have formed him; yea, I have made him. (Isaiah 43:5–7)

But Zion said, The Lord hath forsaken me, and my Lord hath

forgotten me. Can a woman forget her sucking child, that she should not have compassion on the son of her womb? Yea, they may forget, yet will I not forget thee. Behold, I have graven thee upon the palms of my hands; thy walls are continually before me. Thy children shall make haste; thy destroyers and they that made thee waste shall go forth of thee. . . . Then shalt thou say in thine heart, Who hath begotten me these, seeing I have lost my children, and am desolate, a captive, and removing to and fro? And who hath brought up these? Behold, I was left alone; these, where had they been? Thus saith the Lord God, Behold, I will lift up mine hand to the Gentiles, and set up my standard to the people: and they shall bring thy sons in their arms, and thy daughters shall be carried upon their shoulders. And kings shall be thy nursing fathers, and their queens thy nursing mothers: they shall bow down to thee with their face toward the earth, and lick up the dust of thy feet; and thou shalt know that I am the Lord: for they shall not be ashamed that wait for me. (Isaiah 49:14–17, 21–23)

Break forth into joy, sing together, ye waste places of Jerusalem: for the Lord hath comforted his people, he hath redeemed Jerusalem. The Lord hath made bare his holy arm in the eyes of all the nations; and all the ends of the earth shall see the salvation of our God. Depart ye, depart ye, go ye out from thence, touch no unclean thing; go ye out of the midst of her; be ye clean, that bear the vessels of the Lord. For ye shall not go out with haste, nor go by flight: for the Lord will go before you; and the God of Israel will be your rearward. (Isaiah 52:9–12)

For a small moment have I forsaken thee; but with great mercies will I gather thee. In a little wrath I hid my face from thee for a moment; but with everlasting kindness will I have mercy on thee, saith the Lord thy Redeemer. For this is as the waters of Noah unto me: for as I have sworn that the waters of Noah should no more go over the earth; so have I sworn that I would not be wroth with thee, nor rebuke thee. For the mountains shall depart, and the hills be removed; but my kindness shall not depart from thee, neither shall the covenant of my peace be removed, saith the Lord that hath mercy on thee. (Isaiah 54:7–10)

For Zion's sake will I not hold my peace, and for Jerusalem's sake I will not rest, until the righteousness thereof go forth as brightness, and the salvation thereof as a lamp that burneth. Thou shalt no more be termed Forsaken; neither shall thy land any more be termed Desolate: but . . . give him no rest, till he establish, and till he make Jerusalem a praise in the earth. And they shall call them, the holy people, the redeemed of the Lord: and thou shalt be called, sought out, a city not forsaken. (Isaiah 62:1, 4, 7, 12)

JEREMIAH

Jeremiah began his ministry as prophet in Jerusalem under King Josiah, a righteous man whose life was cut short while defending his people against the Egyptians in the Jezreel Valley at Megiddo. Jeremiah witnessed the rapid decline of the kingdom of Judah thereafter, always speaking out about the disasters that would befall the Holy City. For his honest and forthright service as spokesman for God in Jerusalem, Jeremiah was imprisoned, put in the stocks, and otherwise mistreated by the leaders of the Jews. He, like Isaiah, knowing the forthcoming disaster at the hands of the Babylonians, foresaw a day when Jews would return to their own country:

Turn, O backsliding children, saith the Lord; for I am married unto you: and I will take you one of a city, and two of a family, and I will bring you to Zion: at that time they shall call Jerusalem the throne of the Lord; and all the nations shall be gathered unto it, to the name of the Lord, to Jerusalem: neither shall they walk any more after the imagination of their evil heart. In those days the house of Judah shall walk with the house of Israel, and they shall come together out of the land of the north to the land that I have given for an inheritance unto your fathers. (Jeremiah 3: 14, 17–18)

Therefore, behold, the days come, saith the Lord, that it shall no more be said, the Lord liveth, that brought up the children of Israel out of the land of Egypt; but, the Lord liveth, that brought up the children of Israel from the land of the north, and from all the lands whither he had driven them: and I will bring them again into their land that I gave unto their fathers. Behold, I will send for many fishers, saith the Lord, and they shall fish them; and after will I send for many hunters, and they shall hunt them from every mountain, and from every hill, and out of the holes of the rocks. (Jeremiah 16:14–16)

And I will gather the remnant of my flock out of all countries whither I have driven them, and will bring them again to their folds; and they shall be fruitful and increase. Therefore, behold, the days come, saith the Lord, that they shall no more say, the Lord liveth, which brought up the children of Israel out of the land of Egypt; but, the Lord liveth, which brought up and which led the seed of the house of Israel out of the north country, and from all countries whither I had driven them; and they shall dwell in their own land. (Jeremiah 23:3, 7–8)

And I will be found of you, saith the Lord: and I will turn away your captivity, and I will gather you from all the nations, and from all the places whither I have driven you, saith the Lord; and I will bring you again into the place whence I caused you to be carried away captive. (Jeremiah 29:14)

For, lo, the days come, saith the Lord, that I will bring again the captivity of my people Israel and Judah, saith the Lord: and I will cause them to return to the land that I gave to their fathers, and they shall possess it. . . . Therefore fear thou not, O my servant Jacob, saith the Lord; neither be dismayed, O Israel: for, lo, I will save thee from afar, and thy seed from the land of their captivity; and Jacob shall return, and shall be in rest, and be quiet, and none shall make him afraid. For I am with thee, saith the Lord, to save thee: though I make a full end of all nations whither I have scattered thee, yet will I not make a full end of thee: but I will correct thee in measure, and will not leave thee altogether unpunished. . . . Thus saith the Lord; Behold, I will bring again the captivity of Jacob's tents, and have mercy on his dwellingplaces; and the city shall be builded upon her own heap, and the palace shall remain after the manner thereof. And out of them shall proceed thanksgiving and the voice of them that make merry: and I will multiply them, and they shall not be few; I will also glorify them, and they shall not be small. . . . And ye shall be my people, and I will be your God. (Jeremiah 30:3, 10–11, 18–19, 22)

At the same time, saith the Lord, will I be the God of all the families of Israel, and they shall be my people. Thus saith the Lord, The people which were left of the sword found grace in the wilderness; even Israel, when I went to cause him to rest. The Lord hath appeared of old unto me, saying, Yea, I have loved thee with an everlasting love: therefore with lovingkindness have I drawn thee. Again I will build thee, and thou shalt be built, O virgin of Israel: thou shalt again be adorned with thy tabrets, and shalt go forth in the dances of them that make merry. Thou shalt yet plant vines upon the mountains of Samaria: the planters shall plant, and shall eat them as common things. For there shall be a day, that the watchmen upon the mount Ephraim shall cry, Arise ye, and let us go up to Zion unto the Lord our God. For thus saith the Lord; Sing with gladness for Jacob, and shout among the chief of the nations: publish ye, praise ye, and say, O Lord, save thy people, the remnant of Israel. Behold, I will bring them from the north country, and gather them from the coasts of the earth, and with them the blind and the lame, the woman with child and her that travaileth with child together: a great company shall return thither. They shall come with weeping, and with supplications will I lead them: I will cause them to walk by the rivers of waters in a straight way, wherein they shall not stumble: for I am a father to Israel, and Ephraim is my firstborn. Hear the word of the Lord, O ye nations, and declare it in the isles afar off, and say, He that scattered Israel will gather him, and keep him, as a shepherd doth his flock. For the Lord hath redeemed Jacob, and ransomed him from the hand of him that was stronger than he. Therefore they shall come and sing in the height of Zion, and shall flow together to the goodness of the Lord, for wheat, and for wine, and for oil, and for the young of the flock and of the herd: and their soul shall be as a watered garden; and they shall not sorrow any more at all. (Jeremiah 31:1–12)

Behold, I will gather them out of all countries, whither I have driven them in mine anger, and in my fury, and in great wrath; and I will bring them again unto this place, and I will cause them to dwell safely: and they shall be my people, and I will be their God. (Jeremiah 32:37–38)

EZEKIEL

Though a generation younger, Ezekiel was a contemporary of Jeremiah. His prophetic ministry was conducted in Babylon after he was taken captive to what was then the largest metropolis in the world. Jeremiah had predicted the enslavement of many Jews in Babylon and told them to build houses and pray for the peace of Babylon because they would remain there for many years. Ezekiel was called to serve as their spiritual leader in captivity. In this time of sorrow and regret, he taught the Jews that there would be a future return to Jerusalem and a final rebuilding of the temple there:

> Therefore say, Thus saith the Lord God; although I have cast them far off among the heathen, and although I have scattered them among the countries, yet will I be to them as a little sanctuary in the countries where they shall come. Therefore say, Thus saith the Lord God; I will even gather you from the people, and assemble you out of the countries where ye have been scattered, and I will give you the land of Israel. And they shall come thither, and they shall take away all the detestable things thereof and all the abominations thereof from thence. And I will give them one heart, and I will put a new spirit within you; and I will take the stony heart out of their flesh, and will give them an heart of flesh: that they may walk in my statutes, and keep mine ordinances, and do them: and they shall be my people, and I will be their God. (Ezekiel 11:16–20)

> I will accept you with your sweet savour, when I bring you out from the people, and gather you out of the countries wherein ye have been scattered; and I will be sanctified in you before the heathen. (Ezekiel 20:41)

> For I will take you from among the heathen, and gather you out of all countries, and will bring you into your own land. Then will I sprinkle clean water upon you, and ye shall be clean: from all your filthiness, and from all your idols, will I cleanse you. Thus saith the Lord God; In the day that I shall have cleansed you from all your iniquities I will also cause you to dwell in the cities, and

the wastes shall be builded. And the desolate land shall be tilled, whereas it lay desolate in the sight of all that passed by. And they shall say, This land that was desolate is become like the garden of Eden; and the waste and desolate and ruined cities are become fenced, and are inhabited. (Ezekiel 36:24–25, 33–35)

THE HOPE OF THE PROMISE

In addition to the words of the three major prophets of the Old Testament, Isaiah, Jeremiah, and Ezekiel, many of the other prophets foretold the return of the Jews to Jerusalem in a future time. The hope of the promise shines brightly in each of these excerpts from Amos, Micah, Zephaniah, and Zechariah:

> For, lo, I will command, and I will sift the house of Israel among all nations, like as corn is sifted in a sieve, yet shall not the least grain fall upon the earth. . . . And I will bring again the captivity of my people of Israel, and they shall build the waste cities, and inhabit them; and they shall plant vineyards, and drink the wine thereof; they shall also make gardens, and eat the fruit of them. And I will plant them upon their land, and they shall no more be pulled up out of their land which I have given them, saith the Lord thy God. (Amos 9:9, 14–15)

> I will surely assemble, O Jacob, all of thee; I will surely gather the remnant of Israel; I will put them together as the sheep of Bozrah, as the flock in the midst of their fold: they shall make great noise by reason of the multitude of men. (Micah 2:12)

> At that time will I bring you again, even in the time that I gather you: for I will make you a name and a praise among all people

of the earth, when I turn back your captivity before your eyes, saith the Lord. (Zephaniah 3:20)

And I will strengthen the house of Judah, and I will save the house of Joseph, and I will bring them again to place them; for I have mercy upon them: and they shall be as though I had not cast them off: for I am the Lord their God, and will hear them. And they of Ephraim shall be like a mighty man, and their heart shall rejoice as through wine: yea, their children shall see it, and be glad; their heart shall rejoice in the Lord. I will hiss for them and gather them; for I have redeemed them: and they shall increase as they have increased. And I will sow them among the people: and they shall remember me in far countries; and they shall live with their children, and turn again. (Zechariah 10:6–9)

The message conveyed about the future gathering of the Jews in the land of Israel is remarkable. According to what these prophets foresaw, the Jews would come from all over the world. Once the gathering started, it would be rapid, even unstoppable. The rulers of the other nations of the world would participate in the gathering, enabling and assisting the Jews in this miraculous event. Because of the gathering, the land of Israel would emerge from desolation to become a garden-like, blossoming place full of activity, goodness, and happiness. After serving as "a little sanctuary" to His people and preserving the heritage of Jewishness throughout the Diaspora, God promises a renewed covenant with His people as they return to the land that was first promised to Abraham and then occupied by Israel under Joshua. There will be better relations between the tribes of Judah (representing the remnant of the Southern Kingdom) and the Ephraim (representing the remnant of the Northern Kingdom). God promises that the return will result in a permanent land of safety for the Jews.

CHAPTER 7

PROPHECIES FULFILLED

For students of history, it is uncanny how in line with these prophecies events have unfolded. During the waning decades of the Ottoman Empire as it became increasingly obvious that the Middle East would not endure indefinitely under Turkish hegemony, the rulers of Europe became increasingly interested in the Holy Land. The French were the first to send an expedition into the Middle East under Napoleon. He arrived in Egypt just as the eighteenth century was ending, conquering Alexandria and Cairo. Had Lord Nelson not defeated the French navy on the Nile, Napoleon might have made extensive conquests, including Jerusalem.

There were rumors that Napoleon intended to remake Palestine into a Jewish state, though historians generally discount this as, at most, propaganda. Nonetheless, Napoleon traversed from Cairo through Gaza to Jaffa, where he defeated an Ottoman defense force. At Acre, he was defeated and forced to retreat to Cairo. Soon thereafter, he abandoned the entire expedition and returned to France. The army he left behind was ultimately defeated by the British. Ironically, the French and British likely learned a great deal about the Middle East during their sparring in the late eighteenth and early nineteenth centuries, whetting their imperial appetites for more, including the later construction of the Suez Canal. More particularly, the British and French learned how vulnerable the Ottoman Empire had become.

BRITISH EMPIRE

During the Napoleonic Wars in the early nineteenth century, however, none of the European powers could exploit this intelligence. Only gradually, as the Victorian era dawned in Great Britain and created increased stability, could the British Empire turn its attention back to the Middle East. In 1838, Great Britain established the first European consulate in Jerusalem.

A synagogue under Wilson's Arch

Lord Palmerston, then British prime minister, instructed the British consul in Jerusalem to use his good offices to offer protection to the Jewish residents in the Holy City. Because the British (along with the Russians and Austro-Hungarians) had assisted the Ottoman Empire with reasserting control over Palestine against the incursion of Egyptian forces, British consular services had influence with the Ottoman Empire and were therefore of considerable value to Jews in Jerusalem, who were generally not treated justly by the Turks. While Jews and Christians were minorities in Palestine, Muslims were a plurality, not a majority. Jerusalem itself consisted of only a few thousand inhabitants. From an economic point of view, the whole territory was underdeveloped and undersized.

British scientists and archeologists came to the Middle East to explore its ancient wonders. The Royal Engineers first mapped Palestine and Jerusalem in 1840–41. A more thorough and reliable survey of Jerusalem was conducted by the British in 1864, funded by philanthropist Angela

Ancient stonework under Wilson's Arch

View of the rooftops of Jerusalem from the Austrian hospice

Burdett-Coutts, who was interested in finding a better water supply for Jerusalem's inhabitants. Charles Wilson, an officer in the Royal Engineers, led the survey and made the first credible scientific investigation of the infrastructure supporting Temple Mount, including the discovery of the massive arch that supported a road connecting the hills of western Jerusalem (now the Jewish Quarter) with the top of Temple Mount during the second temple period. The top of Wilson's Arch is seen immediately to the left by those looking directly at the Western Wall. Lower portions of the arch are now open to the public through tours conducted underground along the northern extension of the Western Wall.

In 1862, recently widowed Queen Victoria sent her twenty-one-year-old son, Prince Edward, on a tour of the Middle East, hoping to bolster growing British designs on the area as the Ottoman Empire slowly corroded from the inside. Jerusalem enjoyed visits from many European royal families during the nineteenth century. Emperor Franz Joseph of Austria came in

1869, staying at the Austrian Hospice for the Holy Family, which still exists today and hosts overnight guests in the Muslim Quarter.

Franz Josef's brother, Archduke Karl Ludwig, the heir apparent to the Austrian throne, died in 1896 of typhoid after allegedly contracting the disease by drinking contaminated water from the Jordan River during his tour of the Holy Land. It was Karl Ludwig's son Archduke Franz Ferdinand who was assassinated in Sarajevo, which led to the start of World War I.

RUSSIAN INTERESTS

A member of the Russian imperial family, Elizabeth Feodorovna, the sister of the last Tsarina, Alexandra, is buried on the Mount of Olives in the Church of Mary Magdalene near Gethsemane. Born in Germany as a Hessian princess, she was the granddaughter of Queen Victoria. She was considered the most beautiful woman in Europe during the late nineteenth

The Russian Orthodox Church of St. Mary Magdalene on the Mount of Olives

century and was romantically pursued by a number of leading European men, including the future kaiser Wilhelm II of Germany. But she eventually gave her heart to Grand Duke Sergei Alexandrovich, fifth son of Tsar Alexander II. After Grand Duke Sergei's assassination by the Socialist Revolutionary Party in 1905, the widowed and childless Grand Duchess Elisabeth turned increasingly to her religious beliefs for comfort. She eventually left royal life and established a convent in Moscow. Her work among the poor was ended when Lenin had her arrested in 1918 and eventually murdered. She has been canonized as the Holy Martyr Elisabeth Feodorovna by the Russian Orthodox Church. Her remains were brought to the Mount of Olives because she and her husband cofounded the St. Mary Magdalene Convent there.

The Russian imperial family had also built a remarkable collection of buildings just outside the Jerusalem city walls near the Jaffa Gate during the nineteenth century. Called the Russian Compound, the seventeen-acre site was sold to Russia by the Ottoman Empire for the purpose of providing rooms and services for the thousands of Russian Christian pilgrims who traveled annually to Jerusalem (some traveling the entire distance by foot). A convent, consulate, hospital, and several hospices were built on these grounds. The Russian Compound was intended to see to the needs of these Christian pilgrims while they sojourned in Ottoman territory.

Russian Jews, on the other hand, were not assisted by the Russian imperial family, though many of them also traveled to the Holy Land. Viewed by Russian Orthodox tenets as the killers of Jesus, Jews in Russia during the late nineteenth century suffered repeated pogroms and persecutions. This persecution of Russian Jews was a contributing factor in the first two waves of Jewish immigration into Palestine (the first and second Aliyahs), with thirty-five thousand arriving in 1882 and another forty thousand in 1905. Once in Ottoman Palestine, Jews had to look to the British consulate for any government protection they might need because Russian state interests were limited to providing help to Christians.

HECHLER AND HERZL

Curiously, however, it was the decidedly anti-Semitic last kaiser of imperial Germany, Wilhelm II, who unintentionally played a decisive role in bringing about the return of Jews to Jerusalem and Palestine. This part of the story begins in Vienna, in the British embassy to the Imperial Court of Austria in 1885. Anglican clergyman William Henry Hechler arrived to become chaplain to the British embassy in Vienna after failing to secure the appointment he had really wanted: Protestant bishop of Jerusalem, a post that for a time was a shared appointment of the German (Lutheran) and British (Anglican) churches. Hechler's father was German, his mother English. Hechler followed his father into the ministry and inherited his father's interest in Judaism as well. After serving meritoriously in the German army during the Franco-Prussian War and then briefly as a missionary in Africa, Hechler recovered from malaria while living with his father, who was a Christian missionary to the Jewish community, in Germany. He became the tutor to the household of Frederick I, Grand Duke of Baden, and uncle to Wilhelm II, then a prince. Hechler found the grand duke to be an avid listener to his "restorationist" (pre-Zionist) theology. Later, while living in Vienna, Hechler became acquainted with Theodor Herzl, leader of the then-nascent Zionist movement.

At the time, Herzl was trying unsuccessfully to generate international legitimacy for his ideas. As a journalist, he had been present at and covered the trial of Captain Alfred Dreyfus in France, who was wrongly convicted of selling French military secrets to the Prussians during the Franco-Prussian War. The anti-Semitism so evident at that trial shocked Herzl and led him to propose a new solution for the Jews in a book titled *Der Judenstaat* (*The Jewish State*). Hechler stumbled upon the book in Vienna, Herzl's hometown, found that Herzl's Zionism matched his sentiments exactly, and sought Herzl out. They became friends and collaborators. Hechler used his contacts within the German royal family to arrange meetings for Herzl with Kaiser Wilhelm II both in Istanbul before the kaiser and the sultan of the Ottoman Empire met, and in Jerusalem before the kaiser participated in the dedication of the Lutheran Church of the Redeemer in 1898.

The international press was invited to document the meeting between the two in Jerusalem. When the private meeting between Herzl and the kaiser in Istanbul became known, the press presumed Herzl had secured the support of Germany and the Ottoman Empire for Zionism. While it was not true that either the kaiser or the sultan actually agreed with Zionism or did any-

The Church of the Redeemer in Jerusalem

thing to materially aid the Zionist cause, the public perception granted the Zionist movement the credibility it needed, both among Jewish communities across continental Europe and in Great Britain.

BALFOUR DECLARATION

Later, after Great Britain survived the perils of World War I while the Russian, Austrian, German, and Ottoman dynasties all failed, there was no international power that could deny Great Britain's Zionist leadership its opportunity to support the creation of a Jewish homeland, as articulated in the Balfour Declaration, which was published a year before the end of the war and read: "His Majesty's government view with favour the establishment in Palestine of a national home for the Jewish people, and will use their best endeavours to facilitate the achievement of this object, it being clearly understood that nothing shall be done which may prejudice

View of the Jezreel Valley from Megiddo

Ancient gate into Megiddo

the civil and religious rights of existing non-Jewish communities in Palestine, or the rights and political status enjoyed by Jews in any other country."

Immediately after the issuance of the Balfour Declaration, British troops won the battle of Megiddo, essentially putting an end to the Ottoman Empire and opening the door for thousands of Jews to emigrate to Palestine.

THE END OF WORLD WAR I

With the end of World War I came a massive realignment of nations and boundaries around the world, creating societal conflicts that led directly to World War II two decades later and which still linger with us today. Out of the remnants of three empires (German, Austro-Hungarian, and Russian) nine new countries were formed in eastern Europe (Finland, Latvia, Lithuania, Estonia, Poland, Czechoslovakia, Austria, Hungary, and Yugoslavia). Most included a single dominant ethnicity within new national boundaries, fomenting a wave of nationalism that had previously been suppressed. With that renewed nationalism (not unlike today's populist politics) came an explicitly racist variety of anti-Semitism, for a number of reasons. Those people who had lost World War I sought an explanation for the massive carnage of the war without any gain and found it by way of a conspiracy theory: they had been "stabbed in the back" by internal traitors, primarily Jews and Communists, working for foreign interests.

This conspiracy theory was, of course, entirely untrue, but the presence of Jews in prominent leadership with Bolshevik movements in Russia (Trotsky), Hungary (Kun), and Bavaria (Toller) lent the conspiracy an air of authority. The harsh penalties of the Versailles Treaty laid at German, Austrian, and Hungarian feet created an atmosphere of general despair, leading to broad societal anger and division, the perfect setting for the exploitation of conspiracy theories. (Again, these issues are present in the modern world, and we today need to respond carefully to the seedbeds of conspiracy theories proliferating in our midst.) Sadly, 100,000 Jewish deaths were caused by the return of pogroms across Eastern Europe, and 500,000 Jews were driven from their homes. As a consequence, there was another wave of Jewish immigration to the Holy Land, the Third Aliyah, with the arrival of 40,000 eastern European Jews who largely settled in the Jezreel Valley, beginning its transformation to the breadbasket of Israel, which it is today.

After World War I, the League of Nations endorsed the Balfour Declaration and gave Great Britain a mandate to govern in Palestine. In fact, the entire Middle East, formerly ruled by the Ottoman Empire, was divvied up by the French and British, creating the national boundaries that haunt the governance of the Middle East to this day. During the approximately three decades of the British Mandate, the Jewish population in Palestine swelled from less than 100,000 to more than 600,000 persons, mostly due to in-migration. At the same time, the Palestinian population grew from approximately 600,000 persons to nearly two million. There is no agreement about whether the growth in the Palestinian population was due to only natural increase or whether significant numbers of Muslims arrived from elsewhere. It is clear that Jewish migration substantially improved agricultural and economic conditions for both Jews and Palestinian Arabs.

THE AFTERMATH OF WORLD WAR II

World War II was disastrous for European Jews, with their entire way of life completely eliminated. The Holocaust is memorialized now in Jerusalem on Mount Herzl at Yad Vashem (which means literally "a monument and a name," from Isaiah 56: "To them I will give in my house and within my

The grove dedicated to the Righteous of the Nations at Yad Vashem

Part of the exterior of the memorial to the children who died during the Holocaust, found at Yad Vashem

walls a monument and a name better than sons and daughters. I will give them an everlasting name that will not be cut off" (ISV).

Beyond the shock and sorrow experienced at the discovery of six million Jewish deaths in the Holocaust, worldwide sentiment after the defeat of Nazi Germany coalesced around the importance of creating a homeland for Jews where they would have political control of their destiny. British Mandate authorities had restricted organized immigration of Jews into Palestine before WWII after nearly three hundred thousand Jews escaping Nazi cruelty in Europe arrived in the early 1930s. Immediately after the war, the British were not prepared to manage the inevitable conflicts between Palestinians and Jews that would have resulted had they allowed massive immigration of the surviving Jews from Europe, so the ban continued.

At that time, some 250,000 European Jewish Holocaust survivors lived in camps in Central Europe without adequate supplies, clothing, or even water. With international support, Zionist organizations attempted to organize clandestine mass-immigration schemes for these survivors, against British opposition. The largest single operation in this immigration plan, known as Aliyah Bet, has become known as the Exodus Affair.

The *Exodus* was a renamed transport vessel initially built for tourism on the Chesapeake Bay in the United States but was used by both the British and American navies during WWII. It was purchased in 1946 from the US government by Jewish organizations intending to illegally transport Holocaust survivors from Europe to Palestine. After significant retrofitting, 4500 persons were crowded onto the ship in France, and it set sail in the middle of the night in July of 1947 to avoid British naval surveillance. As the *Exodus* approached the coast of Palestine, the British navy forcibly boarded and commandeered the vessel, killing three persons and injuring ten. The *Exodus* was then taken to Haifa, where all on board were forcefully disembarked and placed on three more seaworthy British vessels for transport back to their port of origin in France.

Worldwide news coverage of the refugees on board the *Exodus* captured the attention and sympathy of the international community. In response to the perception that the British had applied excess force, France refused to accept any disembarked passengers from the *Exodus* group who came involuntarily. Britain was forced to remove the Exodus passengers from France and take them to the British sector of Germany at Hamburg for forced disembarkation and confinement to displaced-persons camps under British control. The whole process was bitterly and publicly opposed by the *Exodus* passengers. It was a public-relations disaster for Great Britain, a natural consequence of forcing Jewish Holocaust survivors to be reinterred in German camps.

The United Nations Special Committee on Palestine observed in person the portion of this episode that occurred in Haifa. In November 1947, the UNSCOP report to the United Nations General Assembly was received and accepted, creating a proposed partition of Palestine between a Jewish state and a Palestinian state and ending the British Mandate. Both the United States and the Soviet Union voted for the plan. Jews in Palestine agreed, though they generally felt the land partition was not in their favor. Palestinians universally rejected the plan, as did the entire Arab community of nations. In fact, the Palestinian community had met each step of the Zionist progress with violent opposition, beginning with riots after the Balfour Declaration went public. The surrounding Arab nations backed the Palestinians and threatened to invade any Jewish state that attempted to fulfill the United Nations charter for a homeland for the Jews in Palestine.

THE DECLARATION OF INDEPENDENCE

Six months later, in May 1948, the British left Palestine. Just hours before the British finally pulled out of the country, on May 14, 1948, in what has become known as Independence Hall in Tel Aviv, David Ben Gurion declared the establishment of the State of Israel.

His words, known as the Declaration of Independence, read in part:

The burial site of David Ben Gurion in the Negev Desert

> The Land of Israel was the birthplace of the Jewish people. Here their spiritual, religious and political identity was shaped. Here they first attained to statehood, created cultural values of national and universal significance and gave to the world the eternal Book of Books. . . .

Independence Hall in Tel Aviv, set up exactly as it was on May 14, 1948, the day David Ben Gurion read the Israeli Declaration of Independence

. . . In recent decades [Jews] returned in their masses. Pioneers, *ma'pilim* [meaning Hebrew immigrants coming to Eretz-Israel in defiance of restrictive legislation], and defenders, they made deserts bloom, revived the Hebrew language, built villages and towns, and created a thriving community controlling its own economy and culture, loving peace but knowing how to defend itself, bringing the blessings of progress to all the country's inhabitants, and aspiring towards independent nationhood. . . .

Survivors of the Nazi holocaust in Europe, as well as Jews from other parts of the world, continued to migrate to Eretz-Israel, undaunted by difficulties, restrictions and dangers, and never ceased to assert their right to a life of dignity, freedom and honest toil in their national homeland. . . .

. . . This recognition by the United Nations of the right of the Jewish people to establish their State is irrevocable.

This right is the natural right of the Jewish people to be masters of their own fate, like all other nations, in their own sovereign State. . . .

The State of Israel will be open for Jewish immigration and for the Ingathering of the Exiles; it will foster the development of the country for the benefit of all its inhabitants; it will be based on freedom, justice and peace as envisaged by the prophets of Israel; it will ensure complete equality of social and political rights to all its inhabitants irrespective of religion, race or sex; it will guarantee freedom of religion, conscience, language, education and culture; it will safeguard the Holy Places of all religions; and it will be faithful to the principles of the Charter of the United Nations. . . .

Placing our trust in the "Rock of Israel," we affix our signatures to this proclamation at this session of the provisional council of state, on the soil of the homeland, in the city of Tel-Aviv, on this Sabbath Eve, the 14th of May, 1948.

What exactly was meant by the term "Rock of Israel" was a matter of some controversy in 1948 and likely remains so today. Some of the signatories to the Declaration of Independence were practicing Orthodox Jews. They clearly intended this phrase to be a reference to the God of Abraham, Isaac, and Jacob, as it was used by King David in his final statement (see 2 Samuel 23:3) or by Isaiah: "Ye shall have a song, as in the night when a holy solemnity is kept; and gladness of heart, as when one goeth with a pipe to come into the mountain of the Lord, to the mighty One of Israel" (Isaiah 30:29). The Hebrew word translated in the King James Version, quoted here as "mighty One" is the word for rock. These Orthodox Jewish leaders of the nascent State of Israel placed their trust in God as they began their new national experience.

David Ben Gurion and others, however, who were also signatories to the Declaration of Independence, were atheists and opposed to any reference to God in this founding document of the State of Israel. For them, the term "Rock of Israel" referred to the common Jewish cultural experience and/or the Israeli Defense Force, both of which they trusted to bring about and protect a successful new nation.

The proclamation also appealed to the Palestinian and Arab communities—which were already on the attack against the Jews—to preserve peace and join together to build up the new State of Israel and the entire Middle East. Sadly, all appeals by the Jewish community to their neighbors for peace and shared prosperity over the years have been rejected. Violence by Muslims against Jews began with the Balfour Declaration and the arrival of the British Mandate governance. As increasing numbers of Jews were allowed to emigrate to Palestine, increasing violence was used by Palestinians in an attempt to deter the migration, ultimately persuading the British, both before and after World War II, to refuse legal Jewish emigration in any numbers. There were, of course, Jewish groups that perpetrated violence in return, including Irgun, which blew up the King David Hotel in Jerusalem after WWII. In fact, the British decision to leave Palestine altogether and abandon the mandate was based upon the realization that British police were in an impossible situation as the targets of violence from both Palestinians and Jews. British foreign policy seemed to swing in favor of the surrounding Arab states, from which Great Britain hoped to receive favorable petroleum-purchasing opportunities, and away from assisting the Jewish population in Palestine. Thus, Great Britain not only forbade any further Jewish in-migration, it also refused to allow Jewish groups in Palestine to arm themselves against an increasingly violent Palestinian and Arab presence.

Once the United Nations declared an end to the British Mandate and proposed a two-state solution to the Palestine problem, civil war erupted in Palestine. Supported by surrounding Arab states, Palestinian Arab militias began attacking Jewish citizens and settlements. Jewish militias fought back using guerilla tactics. From November 1947, when the UN resolution was passed, until the spring of 1948, this ethnic civil war raged with the British Mandate government nominally in control of Palestine but practically unable to rule. British foreign policy, however, was decidedly in favor of the Arab states. Britain sold weapons, including planes, to Egypt and Jordan. These two countries, along with Lebanon, Syria, and Iraq, declared their intent to wage war against the fledgling Jewish state once the British Mandate ended and British troops were out of Palestine.

Meanwhile, the United Nations, supported by the United States, declared an arms embargo against shipments to the Middle East. This had the unintended consequence of hindering Jewish organizations from acquiring arms. It seemed the United States, after voting to approve the establishment of the State of Israel in November of 1947, was trying to do everything it could to keep Israel from emerging as a new nation and defending itself. In fact, the United States did not enter into negotiations to sell arms to Israel until the administration of President John F. Kennedy in the early 1960s.

When David Ben Gurion, on behalf of the seven hundred thousand Jews in Palestine, read aloud the words of the Declaration of Independence for the State of Israel, the hope of returning home that had burned in Jewish hearts for nearly two thousand years flared brighter than ever. But even as they passionately declared that their long centuries of exile were at an end, the future was uncertain. When Ben Gurion alluded to placing trust in the Rock of Israel, he was asserting the only hope it appeared the Jews in Israel had to survive. The Israeli Defense Force had only just consolidated the various Jewish militias, such as the Palmach, a few weeks previously. Of the few thousand men and women serving in the IDF, many had training in warfare, but very few actually had rifles and ammunition. The IDF had no planes, antiaircraft weapons, or artillery. And five well-armed countries in the Arab community—Lebanon, Syria, Iraq, Jordan, and Egypt—had declared war on Israel. Palestinian Arabs, though they had been long-time friends and neighbors of Palestinian Jews, living side by side, and though Jewish leaders from David Ben Gurion down to local elected officials invited them to stay and help build the new nation, left their homes en masse in order to get out of the way of the expected slaughter of Palestine's Jewish population by the combined forces of the Arab nations. The

IDF soldiers caring for the author's grandnieces and grandnephew at the Palmach Museum in Tel Aviv

whole world expected a second Holocaust and the end of Israel before it really could begin.

MIRACLES

And then, just after midnight on May 15, 1948, as the first day of Israeli independence began, shipments of arms and fighter planes arrived near Tel Aviv—a literal miracle that saved the State of Israel from disaster. Syria and Lebanon had engaged Israeli forces in the northern mountains. Iraq and Jordan had taken the central hills of Palestine, including East Jerusalem. And an Egyptian army was, as in ancient times, advancing up the Mediterranean coast through Gaza. The Egyptians intended to demolish Tel Aviv, the urban heart of Israel, with the Egyptian and Jordanian air forces attacking Tel Aviv. Just as these Arab military forces seemed destined to make short work of the brand-new State of Israel, a group of about two dozen mostly Americans, some of Jewish parentage, managed to fly thousands of rifles and machine guns, millions of rounds of ammunition, and several dissembled surplus fighter planes into Palestine.

This group of men was led by Al Schwimmer, a first-generation Jewish-American who had meritoriously served the American military in air-transport services during World War II. He was not a believing or practicing Jew, and none of his friends even knew he was Jewish, but he was grieved by what he saw of the Holocaust in Europe, including the deaths of many of his own relatives. Al saw Jewish Holocaust survivors living in squalor in displaced-persons camps across Europe and felt that something should be done to help them get to Palestine. He offered his considerable air-transport skills and experience to international Jewish groups, thinking he could fly European Jews into Palestine. Instead, he was asked to organize an air force and air transport for weapons past the international embargo into Jewish Palestine.

The surplus military planes, both transports and bombers, were acquired in the United States. Al Schwimmer found pilots, radio operators, mechanics, and logistics workers from among his circle of military contacts. To escape FBI surveillance, he contracted with Panamanian authorities to move his planes to Central America and start a Panamanian national airline. After registering his planes with Panama, however, he flew them across the Atlantic Ocean and into Europe because rifles, machine guns, ammunition, and surplus fighter planes had been located behind the Iron Curtain in Czechoslovakia.

On the very day Schwimmer's air force arrived in Palestine with these desperately-needed weapons, they were used to arm the IDF. Four surplus German fighter planes flown by Schwimmer's pilots attacked the Egyptian army column six miles from Tel Aviv and stopped its advance. What followed was months of savage fighting. The Israeli War of Independence didn't end until March 1949, when the Israelis captured the Negev Desert and reached the Red Sea at Eilat, Israel's southernmost town.

Israel signed armistice agreements with each of the Arab nations that had attacked it and maintained control of a larger area of land than had been initially anticipated by the proposed UN partition. The Gaza Strip and the West Bank, however, were occupied respectively by Egypt and Jordan. In the three years following the war, seven hundred thousand more Jews immigrated to Israel. This included thousands of Holocaust survivors, as well as many from various Arab countries where anti-Jewish hostility had been incited by the Arab losses during the war.

The statue commemorating the Israeli victory capturing Eilat in March of 1949, which ended the Israeli War of Independence

This influx of Jews to the new nation of Israel represented a doubling of its population. All these arrivals were absorbed into society, found jobs and housing, and began participating in the only liberal democracy successfully founded in the Middle East. A similar number of Palestinian Arabs were displaced from their homes in Palestine during the war. However, they were never absorbed into an Arab country despite the fact that Arab societies across the Middle East were far wealthier and many times more populous than was Israel at that time. To this day, the Palestinian refugee population remains stateless and unintegrated into any Muslim country.

TENSIONS IN THE EARLY YEARS

For several years after the 1948 War of Independence, anti-Israeli sentiment was stoked in Egypt by its president Gamal Abdel Nasser. In July of 1956, Nasser seized control of the Suez Canal from the French and British, threatening their military and economic interests in the region. At the same time, Nasser closed both the canal and the Straits of Tiran to Israeli shipping and blockaded the Gulf of Aqaba in violation of international agreements and treaties.

Israel approached France and Great Britain with a plan to attack Egypt. France had already been selling weapons and military supplies to Israel and was therefore a natural ally. In 1956, Israel, France, and Great Britain attacked Egypt, intending to regain western control of the Suez Canal. However, international pressure forced the three invaders to withdraw. Although the result was considered a coalition military victory, with Israel regaining its shipping rights, Nasser won the PR battle and came out the conflict politically strengthened. Britain and France suffered political damage, and many see the Suez Crisis as the effectual end of Great Britain as an international major power.

Nasser once again threatened Israeli shipping near the Sinai Peninsula in the 1960s, culminating in his removal of UN peacekeeping forces and closing the Straits of Tiran on May 22, 1967, which Israel considered an act of war. In June, Israel preemptively attacked and destroyed the Egyptian air force. The Six-Day War that followed against Egypt, Syria, Jordan, Iraq, and Lebanon was an unqualified success for Israel, which captured the Gaza Strip, the Sinai Peninsula, the West Bank, East Jerusalem, and the Golan Heights. Three hundred thousand Palestinians fled the West Bank, and one hundred thousand Syrians were displaced from the Golan Heights. Again, Jewish communities elsewhere in the Arab world faced violent retaliation, and many were expelled and ended up immigrating to Israel.

In 1973, Israel was simultaneously attacked by Egypt (in the Sinai) and Syria (on the Golan Heights) during what became known as the Yom Kippur War. The attack, which began on that holiest day of the Jewish calendar, caught the IDF by surprise. Fierce fighting erupted in both areas, with Israel only barely managing to escape catastrophic damage. The largest tank battle since World War II occurred between the IDF and the Syrian army in the Golan Heights, where a massively outnumbered (five to one) IDF managed to hold their position against Syrian troops. This area in Israel is now known as the Valley of Tears.

The IDF was humbled by the initial success of its enemies during the Yom Kippur War, and Israel changed its foreign policy and began seeking peace agreements with its neighbors. The 1978 Camp David Accords, a direct result of this policy change, led to Israel returning control of the Sinai Peninsula to Egypt, which responded by normalizing relations with Israel in the first recognition of Israel by an Arab country.

Some have commented that Israel would have been better off ceding the Gaza Strip to Egypt along with the Sinai Peninsula. To be fair, it's unlikely that Egypt would have accepted control of the trouble-some area. The Gaza Strip today is

The Valley of Tears

the most densely populated territory in the world, the legacy of thousands of Palestinian Arabs running away from Israeli forces and toward the Egyptian army during the War of Independence. The Palestinian population living in the Gaza Strip has never been offered citizenship or economic participation in Israel. Poverty haunts those living there. Israel has struggled to govern a people who are bitterly opposed to the presence of a Jewish homeland in what they view as their territory. When the Israeli Defense Force withdrew from Gaza, the residents there responded by electing an international Islamic terrorist organization, Hamas, to its governance. Gaza remains one of Israel's most difficult challenges.

Palestinian violence continued to plague Israel despite peace settlements with Egypt, Jordan, and Lebanon. Intifadas, or uprisings, designed to "shake-off" Israeli occupation of the West Bank have flared many times in the years since the Yom Kippur War. These violent episodes eventually caused Israel to build a wall separating many West Bank areas from Jerusalem and other Israeli areas, after which the violence, particularly suicide bombings, subsided. In November 2019, I was in Tel Aviv when rockets were launched from the Gaza Strip, targeting that city. Thankfully, the rockets were intercepted by the Iron Dome defense system, and Israeli life was barely interrupted. The resilience, determination, and underlying goodness of life in Israel under remarkably adverse circumstances is perhaps the most miraculous aspect of the modern State of Israel.

CHAPTER 8

THE CHURCH OF JESUS CHRIST OF LATTER-DAY SAINTS IN ISRAEL

Joseph Smith, the founding prophet of The Church of Jesus Christ of Latter-day Saints, was well versed in biblical prophecy. He accepted the word of the Old Testament prophets, and early in his ministry focused on the anticipated return of the Jews to the Holy Land. He recorded in his history that when he was first visited by Moroni, an ancient American prophet, Moroni quoted several verses of Old Testament scripture to him, including this from the eleventh chapter of Isaiah: "And it shall come to pass in that day, that the Lord shall set his hand again the second time to recover the remnant of his people. . . . And he shall set up an ensign for the nations, and shall assemble the outcasts of Israel, and gather together the dispersed of Judah from the four corners of the earth. The envy also of Ephraim shall depart, and the adversaries of Judah shall be

cut off: Ephraim shall not envy Judah, and Judah shall not vex Ephraim"
(Isaiah 11:11–13).

Moroni told Joseph Smith that this prophecy was about to be fulfilled. In
significant ways, the story of The Church of Jesus Christ of Latter-day Saints
in Israel is about that reconciliation between Ephraim, the major tribe in
the Northern Kingdom, and Judah, which dominated in the Southern
Kingdom, after the two kingdoms split apart upon the death of King Solomon. Members of The Church of Jesus Christ of Latter-day Saints have
been taught that the Restoration of the gospel is a task for members of the
tribe of Ephraim.

Joseph Fielding Smith, grandnephew of Joseph Smith and himself a
prophet and president of the Church, said, "The members of the Church,
most of us of the tribe of Ephraim, are of the remnant of Jacob. We know it
to be the fact that the Lord called upon the descendants of Ephraim to
commence his work in the earth in these last days. We know further that he
has said that he set Ephraim, according to the promises of his birthright,
at the head. Ephraim receives the 'richer blessings,' these blessings being
those of presidency or direction. The keys are with Ephraim" (*Doctrines of
Salvation* 2:250–51).

ORSON HYDE'S DEDICATORY PRAYER

One of the early converts to The Church of Jesus Christ of Latter-day Saints
was Orson Hyde, a man Joseph's age who later became President of the
Quorum of the Twelve Apostles. As early as 1831, right after Hyde's baptism, Joseph Smith told Orson: "Thou shalt go to Jerusalem . . . and be a
watchman unto the house of Israel; and by thy hands shall the Most High
do a great work, which shall prepare the way and greatly facilitate the gathering together of that people" (*History of the Church*, 4:375).

In 1836, just two years before Great Britain opened the first foreign
consulate in Jerusalem, when Joseph reestablished temple worship as a

central spiritual practice among God's people, he prayed during the dedication of that first temple in Kirtland: "We therefore ask thee to have mercy upon the children of Jacob, that Jerusalem, from this hour, may begin to be redeemed; and the yoke of bondage may begin to be broken off from the house of David; and the children of Judah may begin to return to the lands which thou didst give to Abraham, their father" (D&C 109:62–64).

But Joseph Smith did not express his interest in Jerusalem through prayer alone. He extended a call to Orson Hyde in 1835 to serve in the Quorum of the Twelve Apostles. Though at one point Orson wavered in his support of Joseph Smith, by 1840 he had resumed his apostolic labors. In March of that year, in Nauvoo, he went to bed one night, started thinking about "the field of [his] future labors," and a vision was opened before him. For the next six hours, he did not close his eyes as he saw, among other things, "the cities of London, Amsterdam, Constantinople and Jerusalem" (*History of the Church*, 4:375–76). During the vision, Hyde was commanded to go to the cities he was shown. At the next conference of the Church, he was called on that mission and left Nauvoo about a week later, on April 15, 1840. While preaching at a public meeting in Philadelphia, Hyde declared he was on a mission to Jerusalem so he could dedicate that land for the gathering of the Jews.

Once he reached Jerusalem, Hyde completed the business the Lord had called him to the Holy City to conduct. Before sunrise on October 24, 1841, he walked through the just-opened city gates, crossed the Kidron Valley, and climbed the Mount of Olives. There, he offered up a prayer he had already composed for the occasion, which reads in part:

> Thy servant has been obedient to the heavenly vision which Thou gavest him in his native land; and under the shadow of Thine outstretched arm, he has safely arrived in this place to dedicate and consecrate this land unto Thee, for the gathering together of Judah's scattered remnants, according to the predictions of the

holy Prophets—for the building up of Jerusalem again after it has been trodden down by the Gentiles so long, and for rearing a Temple in honor of thy name. . . .

. . . Abraham, Isaac, and Jacob have long since closed their eyes in death, and made the grave their mansion. Their children are scattered and dispersed abroad among the nations of the Gentiles like sheep that have no shepherd, and are still looking forward for the fulfillment of those promises which Thou didst make concerning them; and even this land, which once poured forth nature's richest bounty, and flowed, as it were, with milk and honey, has, to a certain extent, been smitten with barrenness and sterility since it drank from the murderous hands the blood of Him who never sinned. . . .

. . . Let the land become abundantly fruitful when possessed by its rightful heirs; let it again flow with plenty to feed the

Orson Hyde Park and Gardens on the Mount of Olives

Orson Hyde Park and Gardens on the Mount of Olives

returning prodigals who come home with a spirit of grace and supplication; upon it let the clouds distil virtue and richness, and let the fields smile with plenty. Let the flocks and the herds greatly increase and multiply upon the mountains and the hills; and let Thy great kindness conquer and subdue the unbelief of Thy people. Do Thou take from them their stony heart and give them a heart of flesh; and may the Sun of Thy favor dispel the cold mists of darkness which have beclouded their atmosphere. Incline them to gather in upon this land according to Thy word. Let them come like clouds and like doves to their windows. Let the large ships of the nations bring them from the distant isles; and let kings become their nursing fathers, and queens with motherly fondness wipe the tear of sorrow from their eye. . . .

. . . Do Thou now also be pleased to inspire the hearts of kings and the powers of the earth to look with a friendly eye toward this place, and with a desire to see Thy righteous purposes executed in relation thereto. Let them know that it is Thy good pleasure to restore the kingdom unto Israel—raise up Jerusalem as its capital, and constitute her people a distinct nation and government. . . .

Let that nation or that people who shall take an active part in behalf of Abraham's children, and in the raising up of Jerusalem, find favor in Thy sight. (*History of the Church*, 4:456–58)

Hyde was not the only Latter-day Saint leader to travel to Jerusalem to dedicate the land of Israel. In fact, LDS leaders from the First Presidency of the Church or Quorum of the Twelve Apostles have rededicated the Holy Land ten times after Hyde originally consecrated Palestine for the gathering of the Jewish Nation. While the full text of Orson Hyde's prayer has

Orson Hyde Park and Gardens on the Mount of Olives

been preserved, none of the other prayers were written down, and therefore only general descriptions of the intent of the blessing pronounced are known. It is clear, however, that as conditions in the world changed and new challenges presented themselves in the spiritual work of the fullness of times, additional blessings on the Holy Land were needed, to which the Lord responded by inspiration given to His prophet on earth.

George A. Smith, Visit to the Holy Land

In 1873, George A. Smith, First Counselor in the First Presidency, was sent by President Brigham Young to the Holy Land. President Smith assembled a traveling party, including Apostles Lorenzo Snow and Albert Carrington (who was at that time presiding over the European mission of the Church), Eliza R. Snow, Elder Snow's sister (who presided over the Relief Society of the Church at the time), Feramorz Little (Brigham Young's nephew) and his daughter Clara, Paul Schettler (who spoke multiple languages and served as the traveling business manager), and Thomas Jennings (whose father, William Jennings, financed the trip). As the group left Salt Lake City, President Brigham Young handed them a letter which read in part: "When you go to the land of Palestine, we wish you to dedicate and consecrate that land to the Lord, that it may be blessed with the fruitfulness preparatory to the return of the Jews in fulfillment of prophecy and the accomplishment of the purposes of our Heavenly Father" (Blair G. Van Dyke and LaMar C. Berrett, "In the Footsteps of Orson Hyde: Subsequent Dedications of the Holy Land," BYU *Studies Quarterly* 47:1, 57–94).

As previously noted, only a few years later, the first Aliyah, or group immigration, of Russian Jews streamed into Palestine. During the trip, all three of the apostolic visitors to the Holy Land offered up prayers of dedication, calling upon divine power to assist the scattered remnants of Israel to return to their homeland.

MISSIONARIES

In 1898, Apostle Anthon Lund was sent on a mission to the Near East. As the Ottoman Empire teetered on the edge of extinction, ethnic violence erupted within its borders. In particular, Armenian Christians, including a growing group of LDS Church members, found themselves under attack. Wilford Woodruff, then President of the LDS Church, sought a way to ensure the safety of these members. He called Ferdinand Hintze, who had served as Turkish mission president ten years earlier, to return to Turkey again as mission president and assigned Elder Lund to accompany President Hintze on his travel to his assignment. They were specifically asked to search out a location in Palestine for the Armenian LDS Church members to colonize. While in the Holy Land and under Elder Lund's authority, President Hintze rededicated the Holy Land for the gathering of the house of Israel.

The fact that there were LDS missionaries in the Middle East late in the nineteenth century can be documented by three graves that can be visited in the British cemetery in Haifa. In 1892, Adolf Haag, a convert to the Church originally from Germany, was serving among a colony of German Christians. He had been called on his mission from Utah, where he had immigrated as a young man. Researcher Nina Palmer's conversations with Haag's descendants and her extensive study of Haag's personal letters reveal that he left his wife and two sons to accept a mission call to the Turkish Mission, writing home to them just before he died: "The gospel is sweet, it is a rich and costly pearl. It is worth all our efforts and sacrifice." In 1895, John Clark from Farmington, Utah, accepted a call to proselyte among the German Christian colonies in Palestine. He fell prey to an outbreak of smallpox in Haifa. George Grau was one of the converts Mormon missionaries taught in Haifa, joining the Church in 1886. He was in part responsible for many of his friends and family members joining him in The Church of Jesus Christ of Latter-day Saints and became the leader of the LDS congregation in Haifa. He died in 1901 at the age of sixty-one and

The gravestone of Elder Adolf Haag in the British cemetery in Haifa

The gravestone of Brother Georg Grau in the British cemetery in Haifa

The gravestone of Elder John Clark in the British cemetery in Haifa

was buried with the two aforementioned missionaries in the British cemetery.

It is clear that the proselyting efforts of the nineteenth-century LDS missionaries in the Middle East were directed toward Christians (in both Armenia and Palestine) and not Jews or Muslims. As is still the case, back then, there were social constrictions limiting the preaching of the restored gospel among non-Christian adherents of monotheism. Just as was true for these nineteenth-century emissaries of The Church of Jesus Christ of Latter-day Saints, we help God best with the gathering of Israel by strictly heeding the direction of our leaders to not discuss the gospel with anyone in the land of Israel.

LATTER-DAY APOSTOLIC BLESSINGS

In 1902, Apostle Francis Lyman, who at the time presided over the European Mission of the Church, was assigned to tour the Turkish Mission. His traveling companion for the tour was Sylvester Cannon, a multilinguist who was president of the Belgium-Netherlands Mission. They arrived at the ancient port of Jaffa in March 1902 and were met by Turkish Mission president Albert Herman. The following week, Elder Lyman offered prayers in Jerusalem, on the Mount of Olives, and on Mount Carmel. He called for the lost ten tribes to be gathered, for the tribe of Judah to return to Jerusalem, and for the land to be fruitful. Not long after these prayers, the second Aliyah occurred, bringing tens of thousands more Russian Jews to Palestine.

The final three apostolic blessings on the land of Israel were offered in 1927 and 1933 by James Talmage and John Widtsoe, respectively. James Talmadge dedicated the Holy Land once, and John Widtstoe dedicated it twice, once in Haifa (he was actually dedicating a house in Haifa as the mission home for the Palestine-Syria Mission and included a blessing for the entire Holy Land) and once on the Mount of Olives a few days later. Both men, like Francis Lyman before them, were serving as presiding Church authorities in Europe at the time of their travel to the Holy Land. Unlike all previous dedicatory prayers, these three prayers were not offered in territory under the jurisdiction of the Ottoman Empire, which had finally vanished into history at the end of World War I. Rather, Elders Talmage and Widtsoe had come to a Palestine governed by the British Mandate, where Jewish in-migration was, initially, encouraged.

Both men offered prayers for the safe return of the Jews to Palestine during the time when Nazi domination of Germany was building toward the Holocaust and World War II. This was a time when many European Jews had the insight, or were inspired, to leave Europe and settle in what would soon become an independent homeland and nation for the Jewish people.

A GIFT AND A CONTINUING FRIENDSHIP

After the repeated violence of the wars in 1948, 1956, 1967, and 1973, when Jerusalem was again after two thousand years governed by the Jewish people, the mayor of the newly reunited Jerusalem, Teddy Kollek, reached out to The Church of Jesus Christ of Latter-day Saints and inquired whether there might be interest in developing a five-acre property on the Mount of Olives as a commemorative park honoring Orson Hyde. Elder LeGrande Richards spearheaded a fundraising effort, and on the 138th anniversary

The BYU Jerusalem Center on Mount Scopus

of Elder Hyde's dedicatory prayer, October 24, 1979, President Spencer Kimball dedicated the Orson Hyde Park in the presence of two thousand Latter-day Saints, including six Apostles.

While they were in Jerusalem for the dedication of the Orson Hyde Park, President Kimball and a number of other Church leaders decided where to locate the permanent site for the BYU study-abroad program in Israel. Elder Howard W. Hunter of the Quorum of the Twelve Apostles had made six trips to the

The entrance for the BYU Jerusalem Center on Mount Scopus

Holy Land in search of property. He had previewed twenty-six possible sites with President N. Eldon Tanner, who chose seven or eight places to show President Kimball. While viewing the last of these possible spots, President Kimball was shown a spectacular view of Jerusalem from Mount Scopus. That particular spot was not available for construction, but, nonetheless, President Kimball felt inspired to choose it as the site for the BYU Jerusalem Center. Somehow, miraculously, approval for construction there was obtained" (Blair G. Van Dyke and David B. Galbraith, "The Jerusalem Center for Near Eastern Studies: Reflections of a Modern Pioneer," *Religious Educator* 9, no. 1 [2008]: 29–53).

It took a year of negotiations for the Church to secure a lease for that particular parcel and three years of effort to change the zoning to allow a building to be constructed. Immediately, the Church began construction work, followed by four years of intense opposition. Orthodox Jewish leaders were convinced The Church of Jesus Christ of Latter-day Saints

Temple Mount as seen from inside the chapel of the BYU Jerusalem Center on Mount Scopus

was building a proselyting center in Jerusalem and bitterly opposed the endeavor. The opposition to the building project was so intense it received international news coverage, including in leading US newspapers such as *Time* magazine, the *New York Times*, and the *Los Angeles Times*.

Eventually, more than 150 members of the US Congress wrote to Israeli leaders in support of The Church of Jesus Christ of Latter-day Saints, Brigham Young University, and the building project. The congressional message was simple: the LDS Church keeps its commitments. A promise of no proselyting had been made by the Church, and that promise was kept. Several years after establishing a commission to track whether or not the "no proselyting" promise was kept, the Israeli government felt no need to further pursue the issue, and the commission was disbanded.

In 1985, then–BYU President Jeffrey Holland, who chaired the executive committee overseeing the construction project, heard that a minority orthodox party in the Israeli Knesset was intending to bring down the

The BYU Jerusalem Center as seen from across the Kidron Valley

The west patio of the BYU Jerusalem Center

government because it opposed having "the Mormons on Mount Scopus." A new government might very well upset the delicate balance of power and have the unintended consequence of thrusting Israel into war, in effect making the BYU Jerusalem Center an issue that might cause another armed conflict in the Middle East. Once made aware of the situation, President Ezra Taft Benson, during a meeting of the First Presidency and Quorum of the Twelve Apostles, prayed for a miracle. The next day in Jerusalem, one party offered its rival an apology, tensions in the Knesset were eased, war was avoided, and the BYU Jerusalem Center construction continued on. After leaving the presidency of BYU when called as an Apostle, Elder Holland later said: "The miracle that morning came from the fourth floor of the Salt Lake Temple where a prophet, seer and revelator prayed safety and protection down upon something the Lord wanted done in that land" (Sydney Walker, "Elder Holland Gives an Inside Look to Miracles That Made the BYU Jerusalem Center Possible," *Church News*, October 14, 2019).

After many other miracles, not the least being the fact that not a single antiquity was discovered during the construction project (Israeli law requires that when construction uncovers antiquities, the building project must stop until archeological exploration is completed on the site), the BYU Jerusalem Center was dedicated by Elder Howard W. Hunter, later the fourteenth President of The Church of Jesus Christ of Latter-day Saints, on May 16, 1989. Upon touring the building for the first time, Mayor Teddy Kollek

The author visiting Orson Hyde Square at Netanya College

The tree dedicated to Ezra Taft Benson in Orson Hyde Square on the campus of Netanya College

commented: "You have taken the most beautiful piece of property we could have given you and have done more with it than I thought possible. I consider it the most beautiful building built in Jerusalem in recent years" (LaRene Gaunt, "One Voice, *Ensign*, April 1993).

I can only echo Mayor Kollek's sentiments. Having visited the building many times and seen it from the Old City of Jerusalem across the Kidron Valley, I believe it is one of the most awe-inspiring buildings in Israel. It is visited by thousands of Israeli citizens every year and regularly hosts memorable concerts. It is a blessing from Ephraim to Judah.

Members of the tribe of Judah are beginning to recognize this growing reconciliation between Ephraim and Judah. One prominent Israeli who came to personally know members of The Church of Jesus Christ of Latter-day Saints was Joseph Ginat. Born just north of Jerusalem in 1936 during the British Mandate, he lived to serve in the IDF during the 1948, 1956, and 1967 wars. He died in Israel in 2009, having enjoyed a long career in the

Orson Hyde Square, Netanya College, Israel

military, diplomacy, and academia in Israel. He received a PhD from the University of Utah, where he met and became friends with many members of the LDS Church and was a personal friend of LDS prophets Harold B. Lee, Spencer W. Kimball, Ezra Taft Benson, Howard W. Hunter, Gordon B. Hinckley, and Thomas S. Monson. Through Ginat's contacts in the Israeli government, in which he served as adviser for Arab Affairs five times under three different prime ministers, The Church of Jesus Christ of Latter-day Saints was aided in its pursuit first of the development of the Orson Hyde Park and Gardens and subsequently in the construction of the BYU Jerusalem Center. At the end of his life, Joseph Ginat served as a college vice president at Netanya Academic College, located north of Tel Aviv. His final act of reconciliation between the tribes of Ephraim and Judah was the establishment on that campus of an Orson Hyde Square, a garden commemorating the many LDS leaders who have journeyed to the Holy Land to offer blessings of renewal and return. In the garden are trees

As of the writing of this book, the most recent commemorative tree added to Orson Hyde Square on the campus of Netanya College

The tree commemorating the Prophet Joseph Smith Jr. on Orson Hyde Square, Netany College, Israel

dedicated to every prophet of The Church of Jesus Christ of Latter-day Saints and to every Apostle who offered a prayer of dedication in Palestine, from Orson Hyde to John Widtsoe.

The no-proselyting promise from The Church of Jesus Christ of Latter-day Saints to the people of Israel continues to this day. LDS Church services are held in three branches of the Church in Israel: Jerusalem (in the chapel at the BYU Center), Tel Aviv, and Be'er Sheva. During one of my trips to the Holy Land, I was privileged to hear a presentation from a member of the LDS Church living in Tiberias, where, at the time, a branch of the Church was located. She was trying to raise her children as members of The Church of Jesus Christ of Latter-day Saints in Israel but was finding it difficult because of the ban on proselyting. No Church materials, including scriptures, were available in Hebrew, her children's native language. No member of the Church was allowed to discuss anything about the Church with anyone else, including a requirement to forgo answering

The marquee in Tel Aviv indicating the location of LDS Church services

any questions about religion. She felt like her children were required to pretend to the world that there was no such thing as the LDS Church while at the same time trying to integrate into that invisible congregation.

It is as if members of the Church in Israel, like the prophet Mormon in ancient America, are required to "stand as an idle witness to manifest unto the world the things which [they see] and [hear]" (Mormon 3:16) but do and say nothing about them. It is a difficult assignment.

The plaque commemorating the dedicatory prayer offered by Elder James E. Talmage on Mount Carmel

A PATHWAY FORWARD

I believe it is the responsibility each member of The Church of Jesus Christ of Latter-day Saints has to love all of our brothers and sisters regardless of ethnicity, nationality, religion, or heritage. On February 15, 1978, the First Presidency of the LDS Church issued a statement to the world regarding God's love for all mankind, which reads in part:

> Based upon ancient and modern revelation, The Church of Jesus Christ of Latter-day Saints gladly teaches and declares the Christian doctrine that all men and women are brothers and sisters, not only by blood relationship from common mortal progenitors but also as literal spirit children of an Eternal Father. The great religious leaders of the world such as Muhammad, Confucius, and the Reformers, as well as philosophers including Socrates, Plato, and others, received a portion of God's light. Moral truths were given to them by God to enlighten whole nations and to bring a higher level of understanding to individuals. . . . Consistent with these truths, we believe that God has given and will give to all peoples sufficient knowledge to help them on their way to eternal salvation, either in this life or in the life to come. . . . Our message therefore is one of special love and concern for the eternal welfare of all men and women, regardless of religious belief, race, or nationality, knowing that we are truly brothers and sisters because we are sons and daughters of the same Eternal Father.

Nowhere, it seems, is it more difficult to live out that challenge than in the Holy Land, a place revered by all three monotheistic religious traditions. In Israel, fear of offending keeps members of The Church of Jesus Christ of Latter-day Saints silent. While we embrace the ongoing reconciliation between the tribes of Ephraim and Judah as prophesied by Isaiah, we do not wish to ignore the plight of others from the family of Abraham who are not Israelites but are from Ishmael or Esau. Biblical minimalists look at the strife created by those who profess love of God and postulate that the world would be better off without religion. For them, there is neither hope nor promise in scripture or the world of the sacred. They live without God in the world and without a sense of the miraculous, which is to say without the sense of what is possible.

In the spirit of offering a pathway forward for all who have an interest in the Holy Land, here are the words of LDS leader Carlos Asay, who served his mission as a young man in Lebanon and Syria just as the modern nation of Israel came into being. He is commenting about what is or can be shared by members of The Church of Jesus Christ of Latter-day Saints with their brothers and sisters who adhere to the Muslim religion, but the point being made is universal:

1. *Prophets and Revelation.* We read in the Qur'an: "We believe in Allah and that which is revealed unto us and that which was revealed to Abraham, and Ishmael, and Isaac, and Jacob, and the tribes, and that which Moses and Jesus received, and that which the prophets received from their Lord. We make no distinction between any of them, and unto him we have surrendered" [Qur'an 2:136].

   In the Latter-day Saint or Mormon faith, a comparable message about revelation is found: "We believe all that God has revealed, all that He does now reveal, and we believe that He will yet reveal many great and important things pertaining to the Kingdom of God" [Article of Faith 1:9].

2. *Golden Rule.* Another similarity from the Qur'an is "Offer to men what thou desirest should be offered to thee; avoid doing to men what thou dost not wish to be done to thee."

   Our LDS version of the Golden Rule from the Book of Mormon

reads "Therefore all things whatsoever ye would that men should do to you, do ye even so to them, for this is the law and the prophets" (3 Nephi 14:12).

3. *Obedience and Works.* One of my favorite teachings taken from the Qur'an deals with obedience and works:

> Righteousness does not consist in whether you face towards the east or the west. The righteous man is he who believes in Allah and the last day, in the angels and the scriptures and the prophets; who for the love of Allah gives his wealth to his kinsfolk, to the orphans, to the needy, to the wayfarers and to the beggars, and for the redemption of captives; who attends to his prayers and pays the alms-tax; who is true to his promises and steadfast in trial and adversity and in times of war. Such are the true believers; such are the Godfearing" [Qur'an 2:177].

This teaching is similar in intent and content to two of the LDS Articles of Faith:

> We believe that. . . . all mankind may be saved, by obedience to the laws and ordinances of the Gospel [Article of Faith 1:3].

> We believe in being honest, true, chaste, benevolent, virtuous, and in doing good to all men; indeed, we may say that we follow the admonition of Paul—We believe all things, we hope all things, we have endured many things, and hope to be able to endure all things. If there is anything virtuous, lovely, or of good report or praiseworthy, we seek after these things [Article of Faith 1:13]. ("God's Love for Mankind," *Mormons and Muslims: Spiritual Foundations and Modern Manifestions*, edited by Spencer J. Palmer, BYU Religious Studies Center, 1983).

Let us join Carlos Asay and seek what is common among us. In modern Israel, we can find the evidence of millennia of man's efforts to find what Paul called the "hope of the promise made of God." What we choose to believe is important. Biblical minimalists choose to believe that miracles don't happen, that God doesn't exist, and that we are not His beloved children and therefore that there is neither a promise nor a hope for us. Travel to Israel can open one's eyes to millennia of human efforts to choose to honor what is sacred. Let us make our belief choices based upon what our highest purpose is, what motivates us to offer to others what we seek for ourselves, and what preserves our sacred obligations to children and others who need us.

CHAPTER 9

THE FUTURE OF JERUSALEM AND THE HOLY LAND

It is an axiom of biblical minimalists that no one knows the future. They deny that Old Testament prophets foresaw the coming of the Messiah. They don't believe the writers of the New Testament, and they don't believe Jesus of Nazareth was the fulfillment of the Old Testament messianic promises. They cannot accept the testimony of the Gospels: that Jesus knew He was to suffer and die so that He could be resurrected and, balancing mercy with justice, offer salvation to all men and women in a fallen world.

And finally, biblical minimalists have voted that the eyewitness accounts of the miracles performed by Jesus, including especially that He rose from the dead and spent more than a month with His disciples, are fictions or legends and not history. These doubters, like King Agrippa, have not been persuaded by the things "which the prophets and Moses did say should come: that Christ should suffer, and that he should be the first that should rise from the dead, and should shew light unto the people, and to the Gentile" (Acts 26:22–3).

Those, perhaps including you, gentle reader, who, like me, have viewed the places in the modern nation of Israel named in the Bible as sites where sacred events have occurred can be blessed by the hope of the promise (see Acts 26:6). They can receive a conviction of all God's promises if they, like Jacob, bring their fears to God and seek to be in the house of His covenant here on earth, the house of Israel, meaning those who prevail with God. Believers see how the prophets of the gathering foretold of the remarkable events that transformed Jerusalem and the surrounding land of promise from a largely unpopulated and uncultivated backwater of the Ottoman Empire into the thriving home of the Jewish people it is today. Just as God fulfilled the promises of the gathering—that kings and queens would hasten the return of the dispersed house of Israel to the Holy Land, that they would come one of a family and two of a city, that He would fight their battles for them, and that the desert would blossom—He will fulfill His promise that as the dew descends upon Mount Hermon and the mountains of Zion, the Lord will command a blessing of life forever more (see Psalm 133:3).

Biblical minimalists have accepted the historical reality of the man Jesus because between evidences of King Herod the Great and Pontius Pilate, there is little doubt that such a man did live. They have read the eyewitness accounts of His life but find themselves unable to embrace any higher meaning in His life and death. Jesus was a mere mortal, they say, who lived an impoverished life, espoused an unusual philosophy He taught those who would listen, but ran afoul of the powers that be and was executed. Finally, biblical minimalists reject the sayings of Jesus that purport any knowledge of the future, including prophecies of His Second Coming.

Luke, for instance, in summary of the final sayings of the resurrected Jesus on the Mount of Olives records, "When they therefore were come together, they asked of him saying, Lord, wilt thou at this time restore again the kingdom to Israel? And he said unto them, It is not for you to know the times or the seasons, which the Father hath put in his own power. But ye shall receive power, after that the Holy Ghost is come upon you: and ye shall be witnesses unto me both in Jerusalem, and in all Judaea, and in Samaria, and unto the uttermost part of the earth. And when he had spoken these things, while they beheld, he was taken up; and a cloud received him out of their sight. And while they looked steadfastly toward heaven as he went up behold, two men stood by them in white apparel; which also said, ye men of Galilee, why stand ye gazing up into heaven? This same Jesus, which is taken up from you into heaven, shall so come in like manner as ye have seen him go into heaven" (Acts 1:6–11).

The prophet Zechariah, certainly known to the inner circle of disciples led by Jesus, places this prophecy about His return in an unusual context—at a time when the nations of the world will be gathered in battle against Israel.

Speaking for the Lord, Zechariah says, "Behold, I will make Jerusalem a cup of trembling unto all the people round about, when they shall be in

The wall surrounding the Old City of Jerusalem, built about five hundred years ago by the Ottoman Empire, seen at the Jaffa Gate

the siege both against Judah and against Jerusalem. . . . For I will gather all nations against Jerusalem to battle; and the city shall be taken, and the houses rifled, and the women ravished; and half of the city shall go forth into captivity, and the residue of the people shall not be cut off from the city" (Zechariah 12:2,14:2).

In the midst of this massive battle for Jerusalem in the last days, two witnesses shall fight against the enemies of the great city, as described by John the Revelator: "And I will give power unto my two witnesses, and they shall prophesy a thousand two hundred and threescore days, clothed in sackcloth. These are the two olive trees, and the two candlesticks standing before the God of the earth. And if any man will hurt them, fire proceedeth out of their mouth, and devoureth their enemies: and if any man will hurt them, he must in this manner be killed. These have power to shut heaven, that it rain not in the days of their prophecy: and have power over waters to turn them to blood, and to smite the earth with all plagues, as often as they will. And when they shall have finished their testimony, the beast that ascendeth out of the bottomless pit shall make war against them, and shall overcome them, and kill them. And their dead bodies shall lie in the street of the great city, which spiritually is called Sodom and Egypt, where also our Lord was crucified. And they of the people and kindreds and tongues and nations shall see their dead bodies three days and an half, and shall not suffer their dead bodies to be put in graves. And they that dwell upon the earth shall rejoice over them, and make merry, and shall send gifts one to another; because these two prophets tormented them that dwelt on the earth. And after three days and an half the Spirit of life from God entered into them, and they stood upon their feet; and great fear fell upon them which saw them. And they heard a great voice from heaven saying unto them, Come up hither. And they ascended up to heaven in a cloud; and their enemies beheld them. And the same hour was there a great earthquake, and the tenth part of the city fell, and in the earthquake were slain of men seven thousand: and the remnant were affrighted, and gave glory to the God of heaven" (Revelations 11:3–13).

I believe that these two prophets who will fight for the people of Jerusalem until they finish their testimony are Elijah, who had the "power to shut heaven, that it rain not" and Moses, who had the "power over waters to turn them to blood, and to smite the earth with plagues" (Revelation 11:6). Neither Elijah nor Moses suffered physical death at the end of their earthly ministries because they were meant to die on the streets of Jerusalem just before Jesus returns to the Mount of Olives. Both were translated after a life of service to God while trying to preserve His covenant people on earth, the very people they will return to serve as witnesses of God. These are the two mighty prophets who served Jesus on the Mount of Transfiguration and who conferred the keys of priesthood service on Joseph Smith and Oliver Cowdery in the Kirtland Temple. As witnesses for three and a half years during the end-of-time battles, Elijah and Moses will undoubtedly be conveying the central message of Jesus, His hope and promise.

Zechariah tells us what that message will be: "And I will pour upon the house of David, and upon the inhabitants of Jerusalem, the spirit of grace and of supplications: and they shall look upon me whom they have pierced, and they shall mourn for him, as one mourneth for his only son, and shall be in bitterness for him, as one that is in bitterness for his firstborn" (Zechariah 12:10).

When Jerusalem is, as Zechariah foresaw, a cup of trembling, under siege by armies of the nations of the world, with the prophets Elijah and Moses having died while defending her, then will come the fulfillment of the prophecy of Jesus given first just before His Crucifixion: "After the tribulation of those days, and the powers of the heavens shall be shaken, then shall appear the sign of the Son of Man in heaven and then shall all the tribes of the earth mourn; and they shall see the Son of Man coming in the clouds of heaven, with power and great glory" (Joseph Smith—Matthew 1:36).

When the people of Jerusalem realize it is their Savior who stands before them, they will mourn for the firstborn of God who died for them at their own hand: "In that day there shall be a fountain opened to the house of David and to the inhabitants of Jerusalem for sin and for uncleanness. . . .

View of Jerusalem from the Mount of Olives

And one shall say unto him, What are these wounds in thine hands? Then he shall answer, Those with which I was wounded in the house of my friends" (Zechariah 13:1, 6).

Zechariah finishes the prophecy by identifying where specifically Jesus will return to the earth: "Then shall the Lord go forth, and fight against those nations [which are arrayed against Jerusalem], as when he fought in the day of battle. And his feet shall stand in that day upon the mount of Olives, which is before Jerusalem on the east, and the mount of Olives shall cleave in the midst thereof toward the east and toward the west, and there shall be a very great valley; and half of the mountain shall remove toward the north, and half of it toward the south. And ye shall flee to the valley of the mountains" (Zechariah 14:3–5).

That is the hope of the promise of Israel. Until the end of time, Jesus will be teaching His people about the grace He has wrought for them. The battle for Jerusalem will be massive, and He will do whatever is needed to win that battle. But, more importantly, He will pour upon His people the spirit of grace and supplication necessary to cleanse them from sin and uncleanness.

He will be a fountain of forgiveness that eliminates the bitterness of all those who have neglected Him, belittled His life, miracles, and Resurrection, or have not believed Him and thereby given assent to His piercing and the wounds in His hands, no matter when it was in the history of the world they lived and made their life's choices on this earth. For those who are physically present at that day when Jerusalem becomes a cup of trembling, under siege, He will clear a path of escape from the armies of the nations of the earth by removing the Mount of Olives as a barrier so that they can flee to His safety.

All who have lived on this earth, from ancient to modern times, have encountered a seemingly impassable mountain while fleeing from one or more of the multivarious threats to human well-being. Mountains of grief, anxiety, illness, violence, depression, guilt, or other woes are the common lot of mankind, often heaped upon us by our own hand. If we, like Jacob, grandson of Abraham and friend of God, lean into a relationship with God when we don't know how to handle the hardships of our lives, if we wrestle with God, we can prevail upon Him for a blessing and, as He did with Jacob, He will bring us into the house of Israel and shower upon us the hope of the promises He has always made and kept. As seen in the ancient landscape still visible in the modern nation of Israel, these promises include: a) the covenant God made with Abraham on Mount Hermon, that what we do individually matters to God and will make all the difference in our own mortal and eternal lives—God gives us meaningful choices, and we are not left to be governed only by natural forces or left to superstition; b) the teachings of Jesus in the Galilee, that our yearning to be free of the compulsion imposed upon us by those more powerful than ourselves and who seek to limit us to a zero-sum world is answered by the much greater power articulated in the Sermon on the Mount, wherein the meek will inherit the earth, the merciful will receive mercy, and the persecuted will rejoice and be exceeding glad because Jesus withstood evil through the Atonement

He wrought for us; c) the covenants of the Sabbath and other feast days of the Jewish calendar, which, along with all Mosaic law and promises, have been subsumed in the new covenant made at baptism and remade at the sacrament table, such that we are awakened to our status as children of God who, through proper attention to our own shortcomings, can be absolved of sin, take the name of our Savior upon us, and enjoy His Spirit to be with us continually. These promises are sure. Despite our trials in this life, with His help, we can have joy and peace. And we can look forward to the promise of our resurrection: "Wherefore, death and hell must deliver up their dead, and hell must deliver up its captive spirits, and the grave must deliver up its captive bodies, and the bodies and the spirits of men will be restored one to the other; and it is by the power of the resurrection of the Holy One of Israel" (2 Nephi 9:12).

And He doesn't promise help only to those who consistently seek Him. While on the cross, He forgave those who nailed His hands and feet to it, a forgiveness that surely applies to those who have minimized His life and message during their own mortality. For those of us in the family of God on earth, no matter how we've leaned away from Christ or for what duration in this life we've made ourselves remote from Him, if we can see the wounds in His hands and pause in our doubts to ask Him about them, He will gift us His grace, move mountains for us, and fight our battles.

It is not for me to know the times or seasons when Jesus will descend to the Mount of Olives and save the citizens of Jerusalem from destruction as prophesied by Zechariah. It is, in my opinion, not important for me to know when that final event will occur. While living in mortality, Jesus was asked on a number of occasions when His Second Coming would occur: "And when he was demanded of the Pharisees, when the kingdom of God should come, he answered them and said, The kingdom of God cometh not with observation: neither shall they say, Lo here! Or, lo there! For, behold, the kingdom of God is within you" (Luke 17:20–21). In other words, the coming of the kingdom of God that matters is an event that happens within your heart.

We are promised there will be an end to the epoch of mortal humanity on the earth. The Second Coming will be a wonderful event, but it is secondary in importance to the coming of Christ within your heart. That is why Jesus will be preaching His gospel to His brothers and sisters until the very end of time. When we embrace His gospel, we hear His testimony—expressed by Isaiah—and we accept it: "The Spirit of the Lord God is upon me; because the Lord hath anointed me to preach good tidings unto the meek; he hath sent me to bind up the brokenhearted, to proclaim liberty to the captives, and the opening of the prison to them that are bound; to proclaim the acceptable year of the Lord, and the day of vengeance of our God; to comfort all that mourn; to appoint unto them that mourn in Zion, to give unto them beauty for ashes, the oil of joy for mourning, the garment of praise for the spirit of heaviness; that they might be called trees of righteousness, the planting of the Lord, that he might be glorified" (Isaiah 61:1–3).

That is the hope of the promise—healing for our broken hearts, liberty from what holds us back, beauty in the face of damaged lives, joy instead of mourning, a feeling of validation instead of loss of promise, and acceptance into the garden of God—I feel when I visit the land of Israel. May those glories be yours in visiting and celebrating the events that have graced human history in the Holy Land, now known as Israel, the place where people prevail upon God to bless them.

ACKNOWLEDGMENTS

Behind every author and book is an army of dedicated people who have helped to make the vision a reality. I am indebted to each person who helped along the way, especially:

Elizabeth Quinn Stewart, my mother's sister, who traveled with me and my mother to Israel in November 2019. Accompanied by our Israeli guide, the three of us enjoyed an intimate ten-day experience in the Holy Land. In advance, Aunt Liz agreed to photo-document our trip and collaborate with me in organizing this book about what one sees and thinks when walking where the house of Israel originated. The photographs she has selected for this book are what any traveler can see in Israel. I offer my gratitude to her for the photographic artistry she has contributed to this book.

I also thank my mother, Alice Patricia Quinn Jarvis, who principally financed the trip Liz and I took to make this book possible. During the trip, my mother shared her most intimate thoughts about Jesus with me, thoughts I will always treasure.

Gordon and Carol Madsen led tours to Israel for decades, teaching the principles of the gospel where it was originally preached. I was blessed to join several of their final tours before their recent retirement, including one they organized for their children and grandchildren. Their soft-spoken yet authoritative approach to scriptural happenings helped me see how sacred events could have unfolded in ancient Israel. I continue to enjoy their gentle mentoring in my approach to writing about and leading tours to Israel.

Nir and Hanna Ganon Nitzan epitomize for me the welcoming, energetic, optimistic nature of modern Israel. They have lived their whole lives in what they describe as the toughest neighborhood in the world, and yet they are irrepressibly loving and upbeat. I have been blessed to visit with them in their home and, in turn, have hosted them in mine. For me, it is easy to see God's hand in their family histories and who they have become.

Once again, Angela Eschler and her team at Scrivener Books have helped me flourish as a writer. For this book, I am particularly grateful to Heidi Brockbank, who is both highly skilled as an editor and wonderfully generous with her time and talents. Michele Preisendorf always effectively applies the rules of style in the final editing of my manuscripts. Thanks to both of them.

My ongoing career as a writer has been made more interesting and enjoyable by my now long-term business affiliation with Melissa Dalton Martinez, my publicist and publishing adviser. She has become a friend and trusted book-business insider.

REFERENCES

Aslan, Reza. 2013. *Zealot: The Life and Times of Jesus of Nazareth*. New York: Random House.

Cahill, Thomas. 1998. *The Gifts of the Jews: How a Tribe of Desert Nomads Changed the Way Everyone Thinks and Feels*. New York: Anchor Books.

Cahill, Thomas. 1999. *Desire of the Everlasting Hills: The World Before and After Jesus*. New York: Anchor Books.

Galbraith David B., Ogden, D. Kelly, and Skinner, Andrew C. 1996. *Jerusalem: The Eternal City*. Salt Lake City, Utah: Deseret Book Company.

Gilbert, Sir Martin. 2014. *Israel: A History*. Np: Rosetta Books.

Holzapfel, Richard Neitzel, Huntsman, Eric D., and Wayment, Thomas A. 2006. *Jesus Christ and the World of the New Testament*. Salt Lake City, Utah: Deseret Book Company.

Holzapfel, Richard Neitzel, Pike, Dana M., and Seely, David Ralph.

2009. *Jehovah and the World of the Old Testament*. Salt Lake City, Utah: Deseret Book Company.

Isbouts, Jean-Pierre. 2017. *In the Footsteps of Jesus: A Chronicle of His Life and the Origins of Christianity*. 2nd ed. Washington DC: National Geographic.

Montefiore, Simon Sebag. 2011. *Jerusalem: The Biography*. New York: Vintage Books.

Talmage James E. 1973. *Jesus the Christ: A Study of the Messiah and His Mission according to Holy Scriptures both Ancient and Modern*. Salt Lake City UT: The Church of Jesus Christ of Latter-day Saints.

NOTE TO THE READER

Thank you so much for taking the time to read *The Hope of the Promise*. If you've enjoyed this book, it would mean a great deal to me if you could leave a review wherever fine books are sold online—and, of course, spread the word!

Please be sure to visit josephqjarvis.com, where you can join my newsletter, learn about events, and get free stuff!

ABOUT THE AUTHOR

Joseph Q. Jarvis, MD, MSPH, has practiced family medicine and organized public-health services for thirty-five years. His spouse of forty-four years, Annette W. Jarvis, is an internationally recognized business-bankruptcy attorney. Together they have five married children and seven grandchildren. Dr. Jarvis is the author of two prior books—*The Purple World: Healing the Harm in American Health Care* and *What the Single Eye Sees: Faith, Hope, Charity, and the Pursuit of Discipleship*. When not busy with his public-health consulting practice, writing, or spending time with family, Dr. Jarvis leads tours in Europe and Israel.